THE EDEXCEL POETRY ANTHOLOGY:
CONFLICT – THE STUDENT GUIDE

DAVID WHEELER

Red Axe Books

ISBN: 978-0993218330

Find us at:

www.dogstailbooks.co.uk

The painting on the cover is a detail from 'Gassed' by John Singer Sargent in response to the First World War.

CONTENTS

Introduction

I hope you find this revision guide useful. It consists of an individual analysis of each poem in the Edexcel Poetry Anthology – Conflict. The analysis of each poem follows the same pattern: there is a section on the poet and the context in which the poem was written and some facts about each author; unfamiliar words are explained; and then each poem has a commentary which focuses on both what the poem is about and the style, form and structure that the poet uses. A final section on each poem summarizes the poem's overall impact and effect. There are no colours, few illustrations, but you will get a clear sense of what each poem is about and each poem's overall effect.

Who or what is this book for?

Perhaps you missed that crucial lesson on one particular poem that you find hard to understand? Good lessons are better than this book, because through different activities and through careful questioning and probing your teacher will help you to arrive at an understanding, an appreciation of the poem that you work out for yourself – and that process is invaluable – it's a process of thinking and exploring as a group, in a pair perhaps and as an individual, and, no matter how good the notes that your class-mates made, those notes are no substitute for having been there and gone through the process of the lesson. So, maybe, through absence, you feel a little out of touch with some of the poems: this book will help you.

Alternatively you may want to read about ideas which you have not encountered in class. Alternatively you may have the sort of teacher who allows you to respond in your own way to the poems; that is a completely valid and worthwhile approach, of course, but it does not suit every student: some students like to have clear guidelines about the meaning of what they read and to have various interpretations suggested to them so that they are at least aware of the overall gist of the poem. It still leaves you free to make up your own mind and have your own ideas, but it does provide a starting point – this book will give you that starting point.

You may be trying to revise the poems in the final days and weeks before the exam and want a quick refresher on poems that you first studied in class a long time ago; maybe it was a Friday afternoon and you weren't paying complete attention; maybe you were late for the lesson and never quite 'got' what the poem is about; maybe you were distracted by something more interesting happening outside and spent the lesson gazing out of the window. This book will help you get to grips with those poems.

It is very unlikely, but you may be reading these poems on your own for the very first time – this book will help you too, because I have assumed that you know nothing about the poem or about poetry, and the commentary on each poem is written so that you can start from scratch. Of course, some of you might find this a tiny bit condescending – and I apologize for that. I should also apologize if there are ideas in this book which are different from ones you have encountered before in class. There are as many different ways to read a poem as there are readers, and each reader might have a slightly different view of a particular poem – as we shall see.

So... if you want a book that tells you what each poem means; comments on features of style and structure; suggests the tone or the overall impact of each poem; gives you the necessary background knowledge to understand each poem – then this is it. At the end you will find a glossary of poetic terms, but after this introduction, there is a commentary on each poem – each commentary is self-contained and can be read on its own. Throughout the book I have used the words that I would use if I were teaching a lesson on these poems – if I use words you don't know or haven't heard, then look them up. Part of education, part of writing well about Literature is the way you yourself write, so to expand your vocabulary is a good thing. Terms which have specific literary meanings are all in the glossary at the back of the book.

Help Yourself!

I hope you find this book helpful in some ways, perhaps many ways. It deliberately does not include very detailed information about the authors for two reasons. Firstly, it would be a waste of space. Secondly, the internet is a rich source of information about writers and their work – an internet search on any of your studied poets or poems will throw up all sorts of interesting resources, including student chat boards, online revision chat-rooms as well as more obvious sources of information like Wikipedia or web sites associated with a particular author. Where there is detailed biographical information here, it is because it is vital to an understanding of the poem.

But do be warned – all the information you can possibly find about a particular poet may help to clarify something you already sensed about the poem, but it is no substitute for engagement with the poem itself. And in the examination the examiner does <u>not</u> want to read a potted biography of the poet whose poem you have chosen to write about. Besides - generalizing from what we know about a writer or his/her era is a dangerous thing: for example, it is important to be aware of William Blake's political beliefs and to be aware that he wrote 'A Poison Tree' and 'The Sick Rose' (discussed in this introduction) during the years of the French Revolution – some might say that without such an awareness the poem cannot be fully appreciated and understood – BUT that will not help you explain the impact of individual words and lines and images at all, nor will it help you write well in the examination. Very often I have started my commentary on a poem with necessary information to help you understand it, but you don't need to reproduce all that information in the exam - it is there to help you fully understand significant details about the poem; to try to reproduce the process of discovery that a good lesson will guide you through. But it probably has little place in the examination.

You may be the sort of student who is doing English Language or English Literature because it is compulsory at your school. But it may also be that as you progress through the course you come to feel that English is a subject that you like and are good at; you may even be intrigued or fascinated by some of the poems in the anthology. If that happens, then do not rely on this book. Look on the internet for resources that will further your interest. For example, if one poet makes a special impact on you – read some of their other work; you will find a lot of it available on-line. Many of the poets in the Literary Heritage sections are now out of copyright – their work is freely available on-line. Many of the contemporary poets have their own websites which can be a fascinating source of extra information and contain links to other poems or biographical information. So there are many ways in which you can help yourself: it's a good habit to get into, especially if you start thinking about the possibility of doing English at A level.

But please remember this is no substitute for a close engagement with the poems themselves. And just as importantly – this book is no substitute for a good lesson which allows you to think about the poem's language and ideas, and then slowly come to an understanding of it. After understanding it (and that is an emotional as much as a logical understanding of it), you may come to appreciate it. What does that mean? Well, as you go through the course and read more and more poems then you may find that you prefer some to others. The next step is to identify why you prefer some poems to others: in this there are no right answers, but there are answers which are clearer and better expressed than others. And preference must be based on reasons to do with the way the poem is written or its overall emotional impact: it's your job to put what you think and feel into words – I cannot help you do that. I can merely point out some of the important features and meanings of the poems. As you grow in confidence and perhaps read other writing on these poems or listening to your teacher or your classmates, then you will start to formulate your own opinions – stealing an idea from one person, a thought from somewhere else and combining all these different things into your own view of the poem.

And that is appreciation. As soon as you say you prefer one poem to another you are engaging in a critical reaction to what you have read – in exactly the same way that people prefer one film to another or one song or performer to another.

Romanticism

In this cluster of poems the first three are designated Romantic poems and it is important that you have an understanding of what Romanticism was. It has very little to do with the word 'romantic' as we apply it today to an event like Valentine's Day.

Romanticism is the name given to the artistic, political and cultural movement that emerged in England and Germany in the 1790s and in the rest of Europe in the 1820s and beyond. It was a movement that saw great changes in literature, painting, sculpture, architecture and music, and found its catalyst in the new philosophical ideas of Jean Jacques Rousseau and Thomas Paine, and in response to the American, French and industrial revolutions. Its chief emphasis was on freedom of individual self-expression, sincerity, spontaneity and originality, but it also looked to the distant past of the Middle Ages for some of its inspiration. In Romantic thought the nature of the poet changed: no longer was a poet someone who could manipulate words well and with skill; the poet was a special individual with a unique vision to communicate and with special insights to communicate through his poetry.

The key characteristics of Romantic poetry in English are:

- a reverence for and veneration of the natural world.
- a belief that the poet was a special person who had important truths to communicate and whose experiences were more intense than those of ordinary people.
- an emphasis on individualism and intense emotion.
- a increased interest in ordinary people – the rural poor and the

urban working classes.

- a political radicalism, best summed up by the watchwords of the French Revolution – liberty, fraternity, equality.
- an overwhelming emphasis on the sensibility and imagination of the poet.
- an interest in medieval and ancient history.
- a veneration of Shakespeare.
- a desire to be original and to reject the orthodoxies of the immediate past.

Of course, not all the poets that we label 'Romantic' displayed all these characteristics all through their careers.

Contemporary Poetry & the Literary Heritage

You will probably have noticed that the poems within each section or cluster of your anthology are designated as Literary Heritage poems. Why? Contemporary poetry consists of poems written in the very recent past by living poets and they are here because as you study English or English Literature, it is felt to be important that you realize that poetry is not dead and poetry is not only written by dead white Englishmen: it is alive and it is being written now all over the English-speaking world by men and by women from a wide variety of backgrounds. So the contemporary poems are there to remind you that poetry is alive and well and thriving. Indeed, as I have already mentioned, many of the contemporary poets have their own websites or perform poetry readings which you may be lucky enough to attend during your course. You can also see some performances of these poems on the internet.

The poems in the first half of the anthology are generally by dead white Englishmen, although there are some poems by women. That sounds dismissive (dead white Englishmen), but it's not meant to be. They are in the anthology to remind you that writers have been writing poetry in English for hundreds of years and that what happens over those centuries is that an agreement emerges about which poems are some of the greatest or most significant ever written in the English Language. How does such agreement emerge? Well, mainly through people continuing to read the poems, responding to them and enjoying them; another concrete way is for the poems to appear in anthologies – which ensures them an even wider audience. The point you need to grasp is that writing in English poetry has been going on for hundreds of years and what has been written in the past influences what is written now. Many contemporary poets will have read the poems that you will read in the Literary Heritage sections. So when you read, for example, 'Exposure' by Wilfred Owen for the first time, you will be joining the millions of English-speaking people all over the world who have read and responded to that poem. Organizations like the BBC have also run public votes where members of the public can vote for their favourite poem – another way that we know which poems are popular. Such poems then become part of the canon. That is not to say, however, that there is only agreement about the value of poems from the distant past: some like those by Carol Ann Duffy and Denise Levertov are from the closing decades of the 20th century; they are included because already there is widespread agreement that these poets are important and influential and that their poems are rewarding to read and study and enjoy.

So part of our heritage, part of the culture of speaking English, whether you speak English in Delhi or London or Manchester or Lahore or Trinidad or Liverpool or Auckland or Toronto or Cape Town or Chicago, is centuries of English poetry and a continuing poetic culture which is rich and vibrant, and includes voices from all over the English-speaking world.

The Secret of Poetry

The secret of poetry, of course, is that there is no secret. Nonetheless, I have come across lots of students who find poetry challenging or off-putting or who don't like it for some reason. I find this attitude bizarre for all sorts of reasons. But some students are very wary of poetry or turned off by it. If you are – rest assured: you shouldn't be!

Poetry is all around us: in proverbial sayings, in popular music, in the nursery rhymes we listen to or sing as children, in playground skipping chants, even in the chanting heard at football matches. All these things use the basic elements of poetry: rhythm and rhyming and very often the techniques of poetry – alliteration, repetition, word play. Advertisements and newspaper headlines also use these techniques to make what they say memorable. Ordinary everyday speech is full of poetry: if you say that something is 'as cheap as chips' you are using alliteration and a simile; if you think someone is 'two sandwiches short of a picnic', if someone is 'a pain in the arse', then you are using metaphors – the only difference is that when poets use similes and metaphors they try to use ones that are fresh and original – and memorable, in the same away that a nursery rhyme or your favourite song lyrics are memorable. Even brand names or shop names use some of the techniques of poetry: if you have a Kwik Fit exhaust supplier in your town you should note the word-play (the mis-spelling of Kwik) and the assonance – the repetition of the 'i' sound. There must be several hundred ladies' hairdressers in the UK called 'Curl Up and Dye' – which is comic word-play. You may go to 'Fat Face' because you like what they sell, but I hope that when you go next time, you'll spare a thought for the alliteration and assonance in the shop's name.

Poets also play with words. So when students tell me they don't like poetry, I don't believe them – I feel they have simply not approached it in the right way. Or perhaps not seen the link between the poetry of everyday life and the poetry they have to study and analyze for GCSE.

Poetry has been around a very long time: the earliest surviving literature in Europe consists of poetry. As far as we can tell poetry existed even before writing, and so poems were passed down by word of mouth for centuries before anyone bothered to write them down. If something is going to be passed down and remembered in this way, then it has to be memorable. And, as we shall see, poets use various techniques and tricks and patterns to make what they write easy to remember or striking in some way - just as you may remember the words to your favourite song or to a nursery rhyme that was recited to you as a small child. Let us take one example. The opening sentence of Charles Dickens' novel *A Tale of Two Cities* is

It was the best of times; it was the worst of times.

It is not poetry, but it is very memorable, because Dickens uses simple repetition, parallelism and paradox to create a very memorable sentence. Parallelism because the two halves of the sentence are the same – except for one word; and paradox because the two words – best and worst – seem to contradict each other. Now look at this recent slogan from an advert for Jaguar cars:

Don't dream it. Drive it.

This uses the same techniques as Dickens: parallelism and paradox (or juxtaposition) and it also uses alliteration. It is all about manipulating words to give them greater impact – to make them memorable.

As I am sure I will repeat elsewhere, it is always vital to read a poem aloud: your teacher might do it very well, you might be lucky enough to hear one of the living poets in the anthology read their poems aloud or you can access many recordings via the internet. I think reading a poem aloud is a good way to revise it: it has been claimed that when we read something aloud we are reading twenty times slower than when we read with our eyes – and that slowness is vital, because it allows the sound of the poem, the turn of each phrase and the rhythm of each poem to stand out. As we shall see, the way a poem sounds is absolutely crucial to its impact – for one thing, it helps you pick out techniques such as alliteration and assonance.

One of the things we will discover is that poetry is partly about pattern – patterns of sounds, of words, of rhythm; patterns of lay-out too, so that a poem and the way it is set out on the page - often separated into separate stanzas (don't call them verses) – is vital. If you quickly glance at a page from the anthology, you would probably assume that what is on the page is a poem – because we have certain expectations of the way that poems look. So what? You have probably been aware for a long time that poets often organize what they write into stanzas. For me this an absolutely crucial part of poetry because as human beings we are in love with patterns, we are addicted to patterns – and that is one of the many reasons we love poetry or find it so appealing. Patterns dominate our lives. We may have patterns on our clothes, our furnishings, our curtains, our carpets. But patterns rule our lives more completely than that: seen from above even a housing estate has patterns – the street lights at regular intervals, the garages and gardens in the same relationship to the houses; a spider's web on a frosty morning; the unique patterns of snowflakes; a honeycomb; your school uniform perhaps; the rhythm of your day, of the timetable you follow at school, of your week, of the seasons and of the year. And where patterns do not exist we like to invent them: the periodic table of elements (which you may be familiar with from Chemistry) does not exist as a table out there in nature – it's the human need to organize and give things a pattern which is responsible for the way it looks. Or look at a map of the world, criss-crossed by lines of longitude and latitude – and invented by the human mind as an aid for navigation.

What on earth has this to do with poetry? Well, poetry, especially from the past, likes to follow patterns and this structure that poets choose is something we instinctively like; it is also important when poets set up a pattern, only to break it to make whatever they are saying even more memorable because it breaks the pattern. We will see this happen in some of the poems in the anthology.

Let us look at it another way. Take the sonnet: if you choose to write a sonnet, you are committing yourself to trying to say what you want to say in 140 syllables, arranged in equal lines of 10 syllables each and fitted to a complex rhyming scheme. It is very hard to do, so why bother? Partly because it is a challenge – to force you to condense what you want to say into 140 syllables concentrates the mind and, more importantly, makes for language that can be very condensed and full of meaning. And, of course, the sonnet has been around for centuries so to choose to write one now means you are following (and hoping to bring something new and surprising) to a long-established form.

So what is poetry? *The Oxford Concise Dictionary of Literary Terms* defines it as:

Language sung, chanted, spoken, or written according to some pattern of recurrence that emphasizes the relationships between words on the basis of sound as well as sense: this pattern is almost always a rhythm or metre, which may be supplemented by rhyme or alliteration or both. All cultures have their poetry, using it for various purposes from sacred ritual to obscene insult, but it is generally employed in those utterances and writings that call for heightened intensity of emotion, dignity of expression, or subtlety of meditation. Poetry is valued for combining pleasures of sound with freshness of ideas....

Remember some of these phrases as you read this book or as you read the poems in the Anthology – which poems have intensity of emotion? Are there some which have a freshness of ideas? Or do some make you think about things more deeply (subtlety of meditation)? Perhaps there are poems which make you do all three? What can I possibly add to the Oxford Book of Literary Terms? Think of your favourite song – whatever type of music you listen to. The song's lyrics will share many of the characteristics of poetry, but the words will be enhanced by the music and the delivery of the vocalist. Is it a song that makes you happy or sad? Angry or mellow? Whatever it makes you feel, a song takes you on an emotional journey – and that is what poems do too, except they lack musical accompaniment. So think of a poem as being like a song – designed to make you feel a particular emotion and think particular thoughts; like some songs, the emotions, the thoughts, may be quiet complex and hard to explain but the similarity is there. And that is another reason why it is important to hear the poems read aloud

– they are designed to be listened to, not simply read. Short poems like the ones in the Anthology are often called lyric poems – and that is because hundreds of years ago they would have been accompanied by music. Before 1066 Anglo-Saxon bards telling even long narrative poems used to accompany themselves on a lyre – a primitive type of guitar and up to Elizabethan times lyric poems were set to music and performed.

Making Connections

As you can see from what is written above, a lot of the work in English on the Anthology is about making connections – the exam question will explicitly ask you to do this. As you study the Anthology or read this book you should try to make connections for yourself. Free your mind and make unusual connections. You might feel that some poems take you on a similar emotional journey; some poems might use metaphor or personification in similar ways; some poems were written at the same time as others and are connected by their context.

If you can connect poems because of their written style or something like structure or technique, then that will impress the examiner more than if you simply connect them by subject matter. The poems are already connected by simply being in the Anthology, so to start an answer, for example, by stating that two poems are about 'Conflict' is a waste of words. You should try to do some thinking for yourself as you read this book and reflect on the poems in the anthology– because it is a good habit to get into and helps prepare you mentally for the exam.

Do you have a favourite word? If you do, you might like to think about why you like it so much. It may well have something to do with the meaning, but it might also have something to do with the sound. Of course, some words are clearly onomatopoeic like *smash*, *bang* and *crack*. But other words have sound qualities too which alter the way we react to them – and they are not obviously onomatopoeic. For example, the word *blister* sounds quite harsh because the letter *b* and the combination of *st* sound a little unpleasant; and, of course, we know what a *blister* is and it is not a pleasant thing. On the other hand, words like *fearful* or *gentle* or *lightly* have a lighter, more delicate sound because of the letters from which they are made. Words like *glitter* and *glisten* cannot be onomatopoeic: onomatopoeia is all about imitating the sound that something makes and *glitter* and *glisten* refer to visual phenomena, but the *gl* at the start and the *st* and *tt* in the middle of the words make them sound entirely appropriate, just right, don't they?

Think of it another way: just reflect on the number of swear words or derogatory terms in English which start with *b* or *p*: *bloody*, *bugger*, *bastard*, *plonker*, *pratt*, *prick*, *prawn* – the list goes on and on. The hard *c* sound in a word like *cackle* is also unpleasant to the ear. So what? Well, as you read poems try to be aware of this, because poets often choose light, gentle sounds to create a gentle atmosphere: listen to the sounds. Of course, the meaning of the word is the dominant element that we respond to, but listen to it as well.

You don't need to know anything about the history of the English language to get a good grade at GCSE. However, where our language comes from makes English unique. English was not spoken in the British Isles until about 450 CE when tribes from what is now Holland invaded as the Roman Empire gradually collapsed. The language these tribes spoke is now known as Old English – if you were to see some it would look very foreign to your eyes, but it is where our basic vocabulary comes from. A survey once picked out the hundred words that are most used in written English: ninety-nine of them had their roots in Old English; the other one was derived from French. The French the Normans spoke had developed from Latin and so when we look at English vocabulary – all the words that are in the dictionary – we can make a simple distinction between words that come from Old English and words that come from Latin – either directly from Latin or from Latin through French. [I am ignoring for the moment all the hundreds of thousands of words English has adopted from all the other languages in the world.]

So what? I hear you think. Well, just as the sounds of words have different qualities, so do the words derived from Old English and from Latin. Words that are Old English in origin are short, blunt and down-to-earth; words derived from Latin or from Latin through French are generally longer and sound more formal. Take a simple example: house, residence, domicile. *House* comes from Old English; *residence* from Latin through French and *domicile* direct from Latin. Of course, if you invited your friends round to your residence, they would probably think you were sounding rather fancy – but that is the whole point. We associate words of Latinate origin with formality and elegance and sometimes poets might use words conscious of the power and associations that they have. Where a poet has used largely Latinate vocabulary it creates a special effect and there are poems in the Anthology where I have pointed this feature out. Equally, the down to earth simplicity of words of English origin can be robust and strong.

Alliteration is a technique that is easy to recognize and is used by many poets and writers to foreground their work. It can exist, of course, in any language. However, it seems to have appealed to writers in English for many centuries. Before 1066 when the Normans invaded and introduced French customs and culture, poetry was widely written in a language we now call Old English, or Anglo Saxon. Old English poetry did not rhyme. How was it patterned then? Each line had roughly the same number of syllables, but what was more important was that each line had three or four words that alliterated. Alliterative poetry continued to be written in English until the 14th century and if you look at these phrases drawn from everyday English speech I think you can see that it has a power even today: busy as a bee, cool as a cucumber, good as gold, right as rain, cheap as chips, dead as a doornail, kith and kin, hearth and home, spick and span, hale and hearty. Alliteration can also be found in invented names. Shops: Coffee Corner, Sushi Station, Caribou Coffee, Circuit City. Fictional characters: Peter Pan, Severus Snape, Donald Duck, Mickey Mouse, Nicholas Nickleby, Humbert Humbert, King Kong, Peppa Pig. The titles of films and novels: *Pride and Prejudice, Sense and Sensibility, Debbie Does Dallas, House on Haunted Hill, Gilmour Girls, V for Vendetta, A Christmas Carol, As Good as it Gets, The Witches of Whitby, The Wolf of Wall Street.* Alliteration is an easy way to make words and phrases memorable.`

So what? Well, as you read the poems and see alliteration being used, I think it is helpful to bear in mind that alliteration is not some specialized poetic technique, but is part of the fabric of everyday English too and it is used in everyday English for the same reasons that it is used by poets – to make the words more memorable.

An Approach to Poetry

This next bit may only be relevant if you are studying the poems for the first time and it is an approach that I use in the classroom. It works well and helps students get their bearing when they first encounter a poem. These are the Five Ws. They are not my idea, but I use them in the classroom all the time. They are simply five questions which are a starting point, a way of getting into the poem and a method of approaching an understanding of it. With some poems some of the answers to the questions are more important than others; with some poems these questions and our answers to them will not get us very far at all – but it is where we will start. I will follow this model with each commentary. They are also a good way to approach the unseen poem. The five questions to ask of each poem you read are:

- Who?

- When?

- Where?

- What?

- Why?

WHO? Who is in the poem? Whose voice the poem uses? This is the first and most basic question. In many poems the poet speaks as themselves, but sometimes they are ventriloquists – they pretend to be someone else. So first of all we must identify the voice of the poem. We must ask ourselves to whom the poem is addressed. It isn't always right to say – the reader; some poems are addressed to a particular individual. And, of course, there may well be other people mentioned in the poem itself. Some poetry is quite cryptic, so who 'you' and 'they' are in a poem make a crucial difference to the way we interpret it. Why are poems 'cryptic'? Well, one reason is that they use language in a very compressed way – compressed perhaps because of the length of each line or the decision to use rhyme.

WHEN? When was the poem written and when is it set? This is where context is important. We know our context: we are reading the poem now, but when the poem was written and when the poem is set (not always the same, by any means) is crucial to the way we interpret it. The gender or background of the poet might be important, the society they were living in, the circumstances which led them to write the poem – all these things can be crucial to how we interpret the poem.

WHERE? Where is the poem set? Where do the events described in the poem take place? With some poems this question is irrelevant; with others it is absolutely vital – it all depends on the poem. In the Anthology you will find some poems which depend on some understanding of where they are set for them to work; you will find other poems where the location is not specified or is irrelevant or generalized – again it depends on the poem.

WHAT? This means what happens in a poem. Some poems describe a place; some describe a particular moment in time; some tell a story; some have a story buried beneath their surface; some make statements – some may do several or all of these things at once. They are all potentially different, but what happens is something very basic and should be grasped before you can move on to really appreciate a poem.

Very often I have kept this section really short, because it is only when you start to look closely at language that you fully understand what is going on.

WHY? This is the hardest question of all and the one with a variety of possible answers, depending on your exact view of the poem in question. I like to think of it as asking ourselves 'Why did the poet write this poem?' Or 'What is the overall message or emotional impact of this poem?' To answer it with every poem, we need to look at all the other questions, the way the poet uses language and its effect on us, and try to put into words the tone of the voice of the poem and the poem's overall impact. Students in the classroom often seem puzzled by my asking them to discuss the poem's tone. But it boils down to this - if you were reading the poem out loud, what tone of voice would you use? What is the mood or atmosphere of the poem? Does the poet, or whoever the poet is pretending to be, have a particular attitude to what he or she is writing about? Answering these questions helps us discuss the tone of the poem. But you may not agree with everybody else about this and this is good: through disagreement and discussion, our understanding of what we read is sharpened. In the commentaries on each poem in this Anthology this question 'Why?' is answered at the very end of each commentary, because it is only after looking closely at the poet's use of language, form and structure that we can begin to answer it. If you feel you know the poem well enough, you might just use the section 'Why?' for each poem as a quick reminder of what its main message is. For all the poems the 'Why?' section consists of a series of bullet points which attempt to give you the words to express what the poem's main point is.

A Word of Warning

This book and the commentaries on individual poems that follow are full of words to do with literature – the technical devices such as metaphor, simile, oxymoron. These are the vocabulary to do with the craft of writing and it is important that you understand them and can use them with confidence. It is the same as using the word *osmosis* in Biology or *isosceles* in Maths. However, in the examination, it is absolutely pointless to pick out a technique unless you can say something vaguely intelligent about its effect – the effect is vital! The examiner will know when a poet is using alliteration and does not need you to point it out; the sort of writing about poetry that consists of picking out technical devices and saying nothing about their effect or linking them in some meaningful way to the subject matter is worthless. I will suggest, in each commentary, what the effect might be, but we can generalize and say that all techniques with words are about making the poem memorable in some away – and this 'making something memorable' is also about foregrounding language. Language that is foregrounded means that it is different from normal everyday language and that it draws attention to itself by being different – it would be like if we all went round every day and tried to use a metaphor and alliteration in everything that we said or if we tried speaking in rhyme all day – people would notice!

Warming Up

Before we look at any of the poems from the anthology, I want to briefly examine two poems to give you a taste of the approach that will be followed throughout the rest of the book. So we will start by looking at two completely different poems. I am not going to subject either to a full analysis, but I will demonstrate with both poems some crucial ways of reading poetry and give you some general guidance which will stand you in good stead when we deal with the poems in the anthology itself. This is not meant to confuse you, but to help. I cannot stress enough that these two poems are not ones that you will be assessed on. They are my choice – and I would use the same method in the classroom – introducing a class very slowly to poetry and 'warming up' for the anthology by practising the sorts of reading skills which will help with any poem. Besides, you may find the method valuable in your preparation for answering on the unseen poem in the exam.

Here is the first poem we will consider. It is called 'Futility' and was written during the First World War by Wilfred Owen about life in the trenches. It links well with his poem 'Exposure' which is in the Anthology.

Move him into the sun—
Gently its touch awoke him once,
At home, whispering of fields half-sown.
Always it woke him, even in France,
Until this morning and this snow.
If anything might rouse him now
The kind old sun will know.

Think how it wakes the seeds,—
Woke, once, the clays of a cold star.
Are limbs, so dear-achieved, are sides,
Full-nerved—still warm—too hard to stir?
Was it for this the clay grew tall?
—O what made fatuous sunbeams toil
To break earth's sleep at all?

Context

Wilfred Owen (1893 – 1918) is widely regarded as the leading British poet of the First World War. He died in action on November 4th 1918 – just seven days before the war finally came to an end. Owen was an officer and was awarded the Military Cross for leadership and bravery in October 1918. The shock of what he saw in the front-line moved him to produce a great many poems in a very short time – most of which were not published until after his death. He seems to have been particularly keen to ensure that the British public was told the horrific truth about the war. He developed his own use of half-rhyme which was to influence other poets for the whole of the 20th century.

'Futility' is one of only five poems that were published when Owen was alive. It was published in a magazine called *The Nation* in June 1918. The compassion that Owen reveals in this poem for the suffering of the ordinary soldier is typical of his work; some of his other poems though, are more brutal and horrific in their realism.

Owen was one of many British writers who felt moved to describe what they saw of the war in the trenches of France and Belgium – and it is a subject to which British writers have returned again and again. Why? Most people would agree that all wars are horrific and cause death and terrible injuries, so what was it about the First World War that so captures the imagination of generation after generation of writers? It seems that the First World War was unique because it caused huge numbers of deaths on all sides without any obvious effect on the course of the war; infantry troops were sent from their trenches to almost certain death and battles lasted for months with only a tiny movement of the front-line – so there was huge loss of life with no clear objective: it began to seem pointless to those involved in it and that pointlessness is echoed by this poem's title. Added to that, the conditions in the trenches – where the men lived and fought and often died – were appalling.

Futility – uselessness.

the clay – humanity. In the Bible God creates man from a lump of clay.

fatuous – foolish

Who? Owen speaks as himself.

When? In the present – *this morning, this snow.* But we know from the biographical context that this poem is set during the First World War –

the poem itself contains no military detail at all.

Where? From the poem we know it is set in France; from our knowledge of Owen, we know that this is set in the trenches of the front-line.

What? A soldier has died. The speaker wants to move him into the sun, since that surely will bring him back to life. It doesn't - and the speaker reflects on the sadness and pity of the death as well as thinking about the bigger questions of human existence.

Commentary

The poem begins with an order - *Move him into the sun* - perhaps given by an officer. A soldier has died in the night – frozen to death in the snow it seems. In a sense, *how* he has died is irrelevant – it is the fact that he has died that Owen finds so shocking. He comes from the countryside and has always woken at dawn – *whispering of fields unsown* suggests that in Britain he worked on the land and had to sow seeds in fields, but this might also suggest the promise for the future growth that seeds contain. Because the sun had always woken him and had woken him *gently*, the speaker articulates an innocent trust that the *kind old sun* will wake him now. But, of course, it won't. The tone of this opening stanza is gentle with soft sounds; even the personified sun used to whisper to the young man.

The second stanza begins by pointing out that our solar system and our planet only exists because of the sun. Owen ends the stanza with three questions that simply cannot be answered without calling into doubt any religious faith and our very existence. Human beings are seen as the summit of evolution – *so dear achieved* – but the poet wonders why Creation occurred at all, if it will end in tragic deaths like this one: the sunbeams that helped create life on earth are *fatuous* and powerless. And this makes Owen question the whole point of human existence. Here in the second stanza the rhythm is broken up by the dashes and question marks which give a faltering, uncertain mood to the poem. Is

Owen bitter or simply puzzled and confused about why we are here on this planet?

This is a very memorable poem in all sorts of ways. It uses half-rhyme to suggest that something very profound is wrong with what Owen describes, but it has no specific references to the First World War – apart from the word *France*. This perhaps gives the poem a timeless quality – it could apply to all deaths in all wars and the sense of futility that Owen feels could be applied to every death of a young person. It fits the definition of freshness of ideas because Owen uses one individual death to question the very nature of our existence on earth, the point of human existence and the nature of God – and he does so in only 12 lines – a remarkable feat of compression. This is a poem that is not just anti-war – it is also, one might say, anti-God because it questions why we are on earth if all that is going to happen is that we will die. It is a tender, poignant and gentle poem, full of a profound sadness at the thought of anyone dying before their time. Nature is important in the poem too: the dead soldier is at home in nature and at ease with the rhythms of nature but that does not help him escape death.

Why?

This short gentle poem raises important issues:

- Life on earth seems pointless when we are faced with the death, especially of young people.

- The sun (which might be symbolic of God as the creator of the planet) can create a whole world, but cannot bring one young man back to life.

- What is the purpose of human life on earth? The poet cannot accept that it is to kill each other in war.

- God – given the questions in the second stanza – seems not to exist or at least not to care about individual human deaths.

Here is the second poem that we will look at as an unseen:

The Sick Rose

O rose, thou art sick!
  The invisible worm,
That flies in the night,
  In the howling storm,

Has found out thy bed   5
  Of crimson joy,
And his dark secret love
  Does thy life destroy

thou – you

thy - your

Who? The voice of the poet, the invisible worm, a rose.

When? In the night during a storm.

Where? Hard to say... in the bed of the rose.

What? Just using what we know from the poem, we can say that an invisible worm discovers the dark secret love of the rose and destroys it during a storm.

It is obvious that this method will not get us very far with this type of poem or, at least, will not get us beyond a superficial interpretation of what it means. Before you read any further, please read my comments below about William Blake's poem 'London', on page 40 because Blake is also the author of 'The Sick Rose'.

What can we say with any certainty about this poem? Its mood is sinister. It is night-time and there is a howling storm. An invisible worm has found out where the rose has its bed and is coming to take its life. *Found out* suggests that the bed needs to be hidden. Paradoxically, although the worm is going to destroy the life of the rose, the worm has a *dark secret love* for the rose: this is now especially disturbing – a love which is dark and secret and which is destructive of life. Not only is it night and, therefore, dark, but the love of the worm is also dark and secret and destructive. We expect love to be a positive emotion which brings good things to our lives.

When faced with this poem many readers want to interpret the poem symbolically – otherwise it becomes a poem about horticulture. The poem is full of words that we associate with love - *rose, bed, joy, love*. In addition, in our culture sending someone roses, especially red roses, is a token of love. But this is a love which has gone wrong and is destructive. Many readers also find the shape of the worm rather phallic – suggestive of the penis. Think of all the types of love which might be considered 'wrong' or destructive. This is the list I came up with, but I am sure you can think of many others:

- Love for someone who does not love you back.

- Love for someone who is already married or in a relationship.

- Love which cannot be expressed.

- Love that transmits disease through unprotected sex.

- Love between two people from different religions.

- Love which is against the law.

- Love which is unwanted by the person you love.

- Love between two people of different class backgrounds.

- Love between two people of the same gender.

- Love or sexual expressions of love which are condemned by the church or by religious doctrine or law.

- Love which is possessive and selfish.

The point of this list is really to show that Blake's power of compression suggests a love that has gone wrong and leaves us to interpret it. To say that 'The Sick Rose' is about any one of the situations listed above would be totally wrong; to say that it suggests them all and encompasses them all, suggests the power of Blake's writing.

Furthermore, if you have read 'London' and its section later in this book and if you remember that the rose is the national symbol of England, then this poem becomes even more than a poem about love gone wrong – it becomes (perhaps) a poem about the state of England and a warning that it will soon be destroyed. You don't have to identify exactly what or who the worm is – the poem does that for you: the worm is destructive and capable of killing – it is a symbol of ALL the things Blake hated in his society. Blake's point is that the rose is sick and is about to be destroyed by sinister, invisible powers.

Finally, if you need any proof of Blake's power to compress meaning, just look at how many words I have used in an attempt to give meaning to his words: Blake uses (including the title) only thirty-seven! This is part of the poem's power and art – that is uses powerful words and imagery from which we can extract a multitude of meanings.

Why? This astonishingly compressed and darkly evocative poem is

- a protest about the England that Blake lived in.

- a protest about the way the church and society saw certain types of love as wrong.

- a warning that love – or what we call love- can be destructive if it is not fulfilled.

- a plea for tolerance and inclusion for those who conventional morality condemns.

Endings

This may seem like an obvious point, one hardly worth drawing attention to, but you have seen from the poems discussed above that the endings of poem are absolutely vital and crucial to their overall effect. In 'The Sick Rose' the final word – *destroy* – carries threat and menace. You will find in many of the poems in the Anthology the ending – the final stanza, the final line, the final sentence, even sometimes the final word – changes what has gone before and forces us to see things differently. So be aware of this as you read and as you revise. When you are writing about poems, the way they end and the emotional conclusion they achieve is a simple way to compare and contrast them. It may not be easy to express what it is exactly that they do achieve, but make sure you write something about the endings, because the endings are often the key to the whole poem. Remember – a poem (like a song) is an emotional journey and the destination, the ending, is part of the overall message, probably its most important part.

'A Poison Tree' – William Blake

Context

William Blake (1757 – 1827) is now seen as the foremost artist and poet of his time, but his work was largely unknown during his lifetime. He was a painter as well as a poet and you can see some of his paintings in art galleries like Tate Britain in London or the Fitzwilliam Museum in Cambridge. 'London' comes from a collection called *Songs of Innocence and of Experience* which appeared together for the first time in 1794. *The Songs of Innocence* (which originally appeared on their own in 1789) are positive in tone and celebrate unspoilt nature, childhood and love. *The Songs of Experience* (from which 'A Poison Tree' comes) depict a corrupt society in which the prevailing mood is one of despair and in which children are exploited and love is corrupted.

Blake was writing at a time when Britain was the wealthiest country in the world because of its global empire and because of the Industrial Revolution which produced goods which were exported all over the world. But not everyone shared in this enormous wealth; the gap between rich and poor was huge, with the poor suffering really terrible living and working conditions. *The Songs of Innocence and of Experience* first 'appeared' (this term will be explained below) in 1794. The date of publication is crucial: Blake is partly seeing London in this way because of events in France. In 1789 the French Revolution began, changing French society forever and ushering in a new age of freedom, equality and brotherhood. Many English people saw what was happening in France and thought it was good to have a society based on greater equality; they looked critically at British society and saw appalling inequalities and injustices. For example, you may be aware that this was the period in British history that some people campaigned against slavery in the British Empire: what is less well-known is that forms of slavery existed in London. There are recorded cases of parents selling their sons to master chimneysweeps in London. The life of a chimney sweep was likely to be short: they were sent up the chimneys of large houses to clean them. Some suffocated; others were trapped in the confined space and died; sometimes their masters would light fires below them to encourage them to work faster – they sometimes were burnt alive. For those who survived, their health was affected: they suffered from terrible lung complaints as a result of breathing in coal dust and, because of poor hygiene, might also succumb to testicular cancer brought on by the accumulated layers of biting coal dust. Apart from being in favour of the slogans of the French Revolution, evidence from his other writings would suggest that Blake was in favour of openness and honesty. Think back to 'The Sick Rose' discussed in the introduction: the rose harbours a "dark, secret love" and is annihilated by the "invisible worm".

Blake had produced *Songs of Innocence* on its own in 1789, although we can tell from his surviving notebooks that he always intended to write *Songs of Experience*. I have used the term 'appeared' because they were not published in a conventional sense. Blake produced each copy of *Songs of Innocence and of Experience* at home by hand and copies were then given to friends and acquaintances. Part of this was Blake's own choice, but we can easily see that his views about Britain and its government would have been highly controversial, so open publication of them may have led to charges of sedition or treason. The British government at the time were terrified of a revolution here, like the one in France, and were doing everything they could to silence people like Blake who were critical of the society in which they lived.

Blake earned his living as an engraver. Before photographs and modern ways of reproducing images, engravings were the cheapest and easiest way of illustrating a book. Blake produced illustrations for other people's books throughout his life – that was how he earned a living. To create an engraving, the engraver has to carve, with a specialist knife, lines on a metal plate; when the plate is then covered in ink and pressed on paper the lines appear on the paper.

On page 33 you can see (in black and white) Blake's illustration for 'a Poison Tree'. Many of the illustrations to Songs of Experience are quite dark in tone and atmosphere, but the overall impression of 'A Poison Tree' is one of light, which, as we will see below, may be connected with the poem's themes and message

Blake used the same technique for reproducing his own poems. After coating the metal plate with ink and producing the outline, Blake coloured each page of each copy of *Songs of Innocence and of Experience* by hand with water colour paint. It is estimated that only 25 copies were produced in his lifetime. If you go to the British Museum you can see one copy: it is tiny and exquisitely detailed and, of course, very personal, because Blake coloured it by hand himself. In addition, to produce his poems in this way was time-consuming and arduous, since in order for the words to appear the right way round when the page was printed, they had to be written in mirror hand-writing on the plate – a painstaking process that must have taken hours and shows not only Blake's artistry, but also his devotion to hard work.

wrath – anger

foe – enemy

wiles – tricks and deceit

stole – crept

When the night had veiled the pole – when clouds had darkened the night sky so that even the Pole Star could not be seen.

Who? The speaker tells a simple story about how his untold anger for an enemy grew and grew until it killed the enemy.

When? No specific time: the poem appeared first in 1794.

Where? No specific location but the metaphor of the tree symbolizing his anger suggests a garden setting.

What? Blake is angry with a friend, tells him so and the anger passes away. He is also angry with an enemy but says nothing. His anger for his enemy grows and grows; Blake uses the metaphor of a pant to describe his growing anger – an anger which he feeds with his hypocritical reactions to his enemy. The tree becomes an apple tree and one night his enemy steals into his garden and plucks the apple. This action ends in his death.

When you first read Blake's 'A Poison Tree' you may be astonished at its simplicity, but as we will see Blake uses a simple form and simple language to make a complex statement about how we deal with anger and its effects.

In the first stanza the situation is clear: the speaker was angry with a friend with whom he was open about his anger and their disagreement, and his anger subsided. He was also angry with his foe, but said nothing, kept his anger hidden and, once it is hidden, it grows. The two couplets are perfectly balanced in terms of rhyme, the number of syllables, the repetition of words and even the exact placing of the caesura in lines 2 and 4.

In the next two stanzas Blake uses anaphora: seven of the eight lines begin with 'and', as he excitedly describes what happens to his wrath. In the second stanza he introduces a metaphor: his wrath is a plant and he 'waterd it in fears' and 'sunned it with smiles/And soft deceitful wiles'. The speaker's disagreement with his friend makes him fearful, makes him cry with rage and frustration, but he still appears outwardly friendly, showering his enemy with 'smiles', showing him to be hypocritical and deceitful.

The third stanza fleshes out the metaphor of the plant which now 'grew day and night'. The anaphora of 'and' does create a sense of excited enjoyment – this is a process which not only involves hypocrisy but the enjoyment of that hypocrisy. The tree grows an apple and Blake tells us:

And my foe beheld it shine,

And he knew that it was mine.

In the final stanza the foe creeps into the garden, steals the apple and dies – a sacrifice to secrecy, hypocrisy and deceit. What is most disturbing is that the speaker is glad. To be glad at someone's misfortune – let alone death – shows an evil and unhealthy attitude.

The poem consists of four quatrains with each quatrain made up of two rhyming couplets. Basically the poem is written in trochaic tetrameters. 'Tetrameter' simply means there are four stressed syllables in each line; trochaic means that the pattern of stresses is a stressed syllable followed by an unstressed syllable. However, Blake uses variations on this basic pattern to reflect what is happening in the poem. Normally we would expect a tetrameter line to have eight syllables – four stressed and four unstressed – but Blake only writes three lines with 8 syllables: lines 2, 4 and the last line of the poem. So what? I hear you say. Well, it means that each line which is short seems a little incomplete and it is masterful of Blake to utilize these short lines in most of the poem – he is describing an incomplete process (the slow and steady growth of his anger (the tree) so he is describing an ongoing, incomplete process – just as the lines themselves are incomplete by being one syllable too short. To further vary the metrical pattern lines 2, 4 and the last line are perfect iambic tetrameters. Why? Because they describe a situation or action which is complete or has been resolved.

The original draft of 'A Poison Tree' in Blake's Notebooks had the title 'Christian Forbearance' suggesting that tolerance for something or someone you disagree with is a good thing, but might also be covering up anger or disapproval. Blake felt that traditional Christians who were taught to be pious could easily be hypocritical, masking their true feelings beneath superficial friendliness. In the poem the speaker's hypocrisy leads to the death of his enemy.

The main theme of 'A Poison Tree' is not anger in itself (we are given no reason for the speaker's anger), but how the suppression of anger is harmful and dangerous. Repressing anger rather than being honest and open about it transforms anger into a seed which will grow into a tree. The growth of the seed is made possible by the energetic anger of the speaker into a destructive force. Blake pursues the metaphor of a growing plant when he writes 'and I waterd it in fears/Night and morning with my tears' his foe makes him fearful and cry tears of rage. The speaker also says 'I sunned it with smiles': on the surface he is polite to his foe and smiles at him. The metaphor works because plants need water and sunlight to thrive. But this deceit and hypocrisy must take its toll on the speaker.

The tree in 'A Poison Tree' is meant to remind the reader of the Tree of the Knowledge of Good and Evil in the Biblical story of the Fall of Man. God forbids Adam or Eve to eat the fruit of that tree, but Eve disobeys and Adam and Eve are expelled from the Garden of Eden. This event is known as the Fall of Man and is responsible (in Christian belief) for bring death and sin into the world. As far as the poem is concerned, the speaker takes the wrathful, vengeful attitude to his enemy – acting in a way that is reminiscent of the God of the Old Testament. [Blake was a devout Christian but his views were rather unorthodox: basically, he thought the God of the Old Testament was evil, but the God of the New Testament – Jesus – was the true God.] In this poem we can say that Blake gives his speaker the attitudes and outlook of the wrathful God of the Old Testament. It may be significant here that the foe is lying on the floor with his arms outstretched – very like the crucified Christ.

If the poem has a message it is not only the importance of expressing your anger and not stifling it. It also demonstrates that the suppression of feelings of anger will lead to a corruption of those feelings, through secrecy and deceit, to a corruption of innocence.

Conflict

The obvious source of conflict in the poem is that between the speaker and his enemy, but there are other more subtle conflicts at work in the poem. Firstly, there is the speaker's own division of the people he knows into friends and foes – we have no knowledge about how he makes this distinction, but it is built into characterizing the people we know as friend or foes. More egregiously there is conflict within the speaker himself, due to his lack of honesty and his superficial friendliness towards his foe – the 'smiles' that he gives the foe and which, in the poem, allow the tree to grow. The effort to be nice to someone he loathes causes the speaker to cry tears which also help the tree and the resentment grow. Therefore, the theft of the apple not only kills the foe, the process leading up to it – the strain and hypocrisy of pretending to be nice to your enemy – takes a psychological toll on the speaker, so that he has lost all human empathy and is glad to see his foe dead alongside the tree.

A Romantic Poem

Blake's work is very different from the poetry of the other Romantic poets. However, the simplicity of language marks this out as a Romantic poem: Wordsworth had experimented with simple language in *Lyrical Ballads*, first published in 1798, and in that collection Samuel Taylor Coleridge's famous poem 'The Rime of the Ancient Mariner' had made use of Christian symbolism as Blake does here. More generally, Blake's call for openness and his criticism of authoritarian power and hypocrisy places this poem firmly within the Romantic poetic spectrum.

In this short but complex poem, Blake:

- attacks hypocrisy.

- attacks secrecy.

- shows how the suppression of anger can have worse consequences than its expression.

- praises openness and honesty in personal relationships.

- by implication attacks the Old Testament God for his harsh, forbidding attitude to humanity.

'The Destruction of Sennacherib' – Lord Byron

Author & Context

Byron was the ideal of the Romantic poet, gaining notoriety for his scandalous private life and being described by one contemporary as 'mad, bad and dangerous to know'.

George Gordon Noel, sixth Baron Byron, was born on 22 January 1788 in London. His father died when he was three, with the result that he inherited his title from his great uncle in 1798.

Byron spent his early years in Aberdeen, and was educated at Harrow School and Cambridge University. In 1809, he left for a two-year tour of a number of Mediterranean countries. He returned to England in 1811, and in 1812 the first two cantos of 'Childe Harold's Pilgrimage' were published. Byron became famous overnight and very wealthy from the high sales his poetry achieved. He achieved what we would now term 'celebrity status', but public opinion was soon to turn against him.

In 1814, Byron's half-sister Augusta gave birth to a daughter, almost certainly Byron's. The following year Byron married Annabella Milbanke, with whom he had a daughter, his only legitimate child. The couple separated in 1816.

Facing mounting pressure as a result of his failed marriage, scandalous affairs and huge debts, Byron left England in April 1816 and never returned. He spent the summer of 1816 at Lake Geneva with Percy Bysshe Shelley, his wife Mary and Mary's half-sister Claire Clairmont, with whom Byron had a daughter.

Byron travelled on to Italy, where he was to live for more than six years. In 1819, while staying in Venice, he began an affair with Teresa Guiccioli, the wife of an Italian nobleman. It was in this period that Byron wrote some of his most famous works, including 'Don Juan' (1819-1824).

In July 1823, Byron left Italy to join the Greek insurgents who were fighting a war of independence against the Ottoman Empire. On 19 April 1824 he died from fever at Missolonghi, in modern day Greece. His death was mourned throughout Britain. His body was brought back to England and buried at his ancestral home in Nottinghamshire.

Much of the Old Testament in the Christian Bible, from which Byron took the bare bones of this story, concerns the efforts of the Israelites or Jews to withstand enemies who wanted to conquer their land or take them into captivity as slaves. This story is no exception. In the Bible the Second Book of Kings, Chapter 18, verse 13 the story begins:

Now in the fourteenth year of King Hezekiah did Sennacherib King of Assyria came up against the fenced cites of Judah and took them.

There then follows an extremely long account of negotiations and diplomacy – which Byron judiciously omits – and the story comes to an end in the Second Book of Kings, Chapter 19, verse 35:

And it came to pass that night that the angel of the Lord went out and smote in the camp of the Assyrians an hundred four score and five thousand: and when they arose early in the morning, behold, they were all dead.

It is this miraculous divine intervention that forms the inspiration for Byron's poem.

If you want to read this poem in context *Hebrew Melodies* is available in a cheap paperback version.

Sennacherib – the main god worshipped by the Assyrians and the name of one of their emperors whose reign was from 705 BCE to 681 BCE.

Assyrian - Assyria was a major Mesopotamian East Semitic kingdom, and empire, of the Ancient Near East, existing as an independent state for a period of approximately six centuries from c. 1250 BCE to 612 BCE, spanning the Early Bronze Age through to the late Iron Age. For a further thirteen centuries, from the end of the 7th century BC to the mid-7th century AD, it survived as a geo-political entity. It covered most of what is now Syria and Iraq.

fold – a fenced enclosure usually holding sheep.

cohorts – troops of soldiers.

host – army.

on the morrow – on the next day.

strown – disordered

waxed – became.

steed – horse.

mail – chain mail armour.

Ashur – another god worshipped by the Assyrians and also the name of one of their major cities and one-time capital.

Baal – another God worshipped by the Assyrians.

The Gentile – 'Gentile' is a Jewish term used to cover all those who are non-Jews, in this case the defeated Assyrian army.

unsmote – 'unhit' by human swords, arrows, lances and other weapons.

Who? Sennacherib besieged Jerusalem in 701 BCE. The speaker narrates a story which is well-documented in the Old Testament. He speaks directly to the modern reader and assumes an air of authority.

When? Byron published the poem in 1815, as part of a collection called *Hebrew Melodies*. The collection was published twice – as a book of poems and also as a book of songs with the music written by the Jewish composer Isaac Nathan.

Where? In Judea, the historic land of the Jews, now roughly covered by the state of Israel and Palestine.

What? The mighty Assyrian army attacks Jerusalem, but is destroyed by divine intervention – the angel of the Lord.

Commentary

The Assyrian Empire was very militaristic and aggressive in expanding their empire. Byron's opening simile 'like the wolf on the fold' – suggests an evil, animalistic aggressor quickly bearing down on an innocent and defenceless innocent. Their troops present an impressive sight: 'gleaming in purple and gold'. The in the third line of the first stanza Byron uses sibilance to give the line cohesion, but the fact that 'their spears were like stars on the sea' suggests the sheer size of the army.

In the second stanza contains an abrupt contrast between the two couplets: in the first couplet the Assyrian army looks grand and magnificent: 'Like the leaves of the forest is green', but in the second couplet and on the morning of the next day the army has been transformed – 'Like the leaves of the forest when Autumn has blown'.

In the third stanza Byron reveals what has happened to the once-mighty army. The Angel of Death has 'breathed in the face of the foe as he passed' and the Assyrians are all dead –

... the eyes of the sleepers waxed deadly and chill,

And the hearts but once heaved, and for ever grew still.

The next two stanzas emphasize the complete destruction of the Assyrian army. In the fourth stanza the horses that carried the Assyrian into battle are foaming at the mouth and as 'cold as the spray of the rock-beating surf'. In the fifth stanza the Assyrian soldiers lie dead wirh 'the dew on his brow, and the rust on his mail'. The mighty army is now all dead and their encampment is destroyed and Byron emphasizes this by describing their camp:

... the tents were all silent, the banners alone,

The lances unlifted, the trumpet unblown.

Despite their military superiority and their wonderful appearance (as suggested in the first stanza) the Assyrian army has been destroyed by the Angel of Death sent by God.

The final stanza describes the reaction in Ashur, the Assyria capital is shown: the widows of the dead soldiers are 'loud in their wail' and the statues of Baal are destroyed in their temples. The Assyrians worshipped several Gods and worshipped idols of them – unlike the Jews who worshipped a single God and who were banned from worshipping statues or idols of him in the Ten Commandments. The materialistic Assyrians have been defeated by the true God – they 'Have melted like snow in the glance of the Lord!'

'The Destruction of Sennacherib' is a very regular poem, consisting of six stanzas each with four lines. Each line has twelve syllables and Byron chooses to write in anapaestic tetrameters. Tetrameter means that there are four stressed syllables in each line. Anapaestic refers to the arrangement of stresses in each line of the poem. An anapaest consists of two unstressed syllables followed by a stressed syllable:

And his *co*horts were *gleam*ing in *pur*ple and *gold*

Here I have italicized the stressed syllables. But why? What is the effect of this metrical patterning? Firstly, when read aloud the poem generates a quick speed which is very appropriate for a narrative poem – the rhythm pushes us on to the next stage of the story. Secondly and more importantly, the speed mimics the speed of the Assyrian army as it approaches Jerusalem – it may even be said to mimic the speed and rhythm of the horses of its army approaching. Thirdly, and perhaps most important of all, the rhythm and its speed suggest the speed of the Assyrian defeat and devastation at the hands of the Angel of Death. In general, therefore, the rhythm helps give us an aural sense of the urgency of the situation facing Jerusalem and the speed at which the events unfold.

The rhyme scheme is AABB: the first two lines in each stanza rhyme with each other as do the third and fourth lines. This apposition of lines is powerful and suggests the opposition between the invading Assyrian army and Jerusalem and its defenders. Byron also uses anaphora at the start of many of his lines – 'like', 'then' and 'and' – 'then' and 'and' are especially appropriate in a narrative poem describing a quick series of events.

Conflict

The conflict in this poem is straightforward between Judea and Jerusalem and the powerful conquering army of the Assyrians. The tone of the poem is one of triumph and celebration at the deliverance from military conquest of Jerusalem and the Jewish people

A Romantic Poem?

Before he published *Hebrew Melodies* Byron was best known for long narrative poems, so to publish a collection of short lyric poems was not typical of him. Byron was also known as a radical free thinker, so it is ironic that he should choose a story from the Old Testament. Indeed, this poem is the most famous poem on a Biblical subject to be produced by any English Romantic poet. Coleridge and Wordsworth were avowedly Christian but neither produced a poem like 'The Destruction of Sennacherib'. Blake, as we have seen, was a Christian but held esoteric and unconventional ideas about God, especially the God of the Old Testament.

And so the poem is not typical of Byron and is an oddity when judged against the work of the other English Romantic poets.

Some readers argue that the arrogance and might of the Assyrian army is analogous to the power and threat to peace posed by the French emperor Napoleon. However, Byron was a political radical and the government of Britain at the time was increasingly tyrannical and oppressive, so if the poem has any contemporary significance, it is probably a reminder to British conservative politicians that their days are numbered.

Why?

In this fast and dramatic narrative poem, Byron:

- makes brilliant use of metre and rhythm to capture both the quick approach of the Assyrian army and its quick and ruthless destruction by the Angel of Death;

- takes a fairly obscure story from the Bible and writes an exciting, thrilling poem whose speed gives the whole poem narrative verve and purpose;

- uses similes well to describe the invading army;.

- at the end paints a vivid picture through words of the desolation of the Assyrian camp

'The Prelude' (stealing the boat) – William Wordsworth

Context

William Wordsworth was born in 1770 in Cockermouth on the edge of the English Lake District. He had a life-long fascination with nature and it is from the natural world that he took much of his inspiration. He died in 1850, having been made Poet Laureate in 1843. Wordsworth began to write *The Prelude* in 1798 and kept working on it and revising it until his death. It was not published until 1850, three months after his death. He published many poems during his own lifetime, but many readers feel that *The Prelude* is his finest work.

This extract is from *The Prelude*, a long autobiographical poem first finished in 1805. It is subtitled *The Growth of the Poet's Mind* – and Wordsworth tells the story of his life, but with the intention of showing his psychological development and also how he came to be a poet. Central to his development, he claims, was the influence of nature: Wordsworth grew up in the English Lake District – a national park and an area of outstanding natural beauty even today. It is not just that Wordsworth liked the beauty of nature – we perhaps all do that because we associate it with peace, away from the hustle and bustle of urban or suburban life; he also believed that nature had a moral influence on him and had made him a better human being. He is at pains throughout *The Prelude* to try and prove this connection – that his experiences in the natural world made him a better person and a poet. You may elsewhere read references to Wordsworth's pantheism. Pantheists worship nature and feel that if there is a God then that God exists in every living thing, every part of the natural world: God is a spirit of the universe which exists in a rock or a daffodil as much as it does in a human being.

her – Nature.

elfin pinnace – a pinnace is a small boat; elfin means small and charming.

covert – secret.

bark – boat.

Who? The poet narrates in the past tense an incident from his childhood.

When? 1805. Wordsworth was a child in the late 18th century, but is recollecting this experience as an adult.

Where? On a lake in the English Lake District, generally thought to be Ullswater.

What? Wordsworth steals a boat and goes for a row on the lake. He explores the ramifications of this incident on his conscience.

Commentary

This extract is written in blank verse. It narrates an incident. This extract comes from Book II of *The Prelude* which is entitled *Childhood and School-Time*. The opening sentence clearly shows the influence of Nature on the young Wordsworth:

One summer evening (led by her) I found

A little boat tied to a willow tree.

We know that *her* refers to nature from the preceding lines. The poet proceeds to unchain the boat and take it for an illicit row on the lake. In effect, Wordsworth is stealing the boat: he describes it as *an act of stealth* (he doesn't want to get caught) and uses an oxymoron - *troubled pleasure* – to show us that he has mixed feelings about what he is doing: he knows it is wrong. Lines 8–11 use a variety of sound effects and very positive vocabulary to present the initial experience of this escapade. He says the boat left behind her

still, on either side,

Small circles glittering idly in the moon,

Until they melted all into one track

Of sparkling light.

Listen to those lines: Wordsworth uses no figurative language, but there is a preponderance of *s*, *l* and *m* sounds which give a gentle, restful feeling which reinforces the meanings of the words. The lines are given more aural coherence by assonance: *side/idly/light* and by consonance - *track/sparkling*. Wordsworth has decided to row across the lake and has picked out a craggy ridge as his landmark towards which he is heading.

This positive tone and atmosphere continues up to line 20. The boat is an *elfin pinnace* – playful, mischievous (like an elf) – and the boat moves through the water *like a swan* – a beautiful, majestic bird.

And then the whole tone changes. By a trick of perspective, as Wordsworth rows across the lake, a huge peak comes into view. When you row, you face the direction you started from and the further Wordsworth rows from the shore of the lake, the mountains behind his starting point start to appear. Look at how the poet describes it and his response to it:

a huge peak, black and huge,

As if with voluntary power instinct,

Upreared its head. I struck and struck again,

And growing still in stature the grim shape

Towered up between me and the stars, and still,

For so it seemed, with purpose of its own

And measured motion like a living thing,

Strode after me.

Like nature, like the boat, the peak is personified and takes on a life of its own, but note also the way a sense of panic in the poet is created by simple repetition of *huge* and *struck*; these lines are full of sibilance too – which creates a sinister, hissing sound. Wordsworth's reaction is one of guilt and shame:

With trembling oars I turned,

And through the silent water stole my way.

He puts the boat back where he found it and then finds he is haunted by this experience for many days afterwards. He does not fully understand what has happened to him:

my brain

Worked with a dim and undetermined sense

Of unknown modes of being.

He is also depressed by the experience:

o'er my thoughts

There hung a darkness, call it solitude

Or blank desertion.

He cannot take his customary pleasure in nature – *No familiar shapes remained* – and his every waking thought and even his sleep is disturbed by

huge and mighty forms that do not live

Like living men, moved slowly through the mind

By day, and were a trouble to my dreams.

How are we to interpret this poem? If some of the language towards the end of the extract seems a little vague, it is because Wordsworth himself – as a small boy – is struggling to make sense of what happened to him.

What is certain is that this experience is a formative one and leads to an epiphany: the poet is made to feel guilty for taking the boat and in that sense it is an important part of Wordsworth's intention – to show that we can learn morality from nature – not just from books or other people. And so nature is presented as beautiful and inspiring, but also frightening if you do something wrong or immoral. The huge and mighty forms that haunt the young boy's mind in the days that follow the incident seem to suggest that there is a divinity in nature, that the natural world (as Wordsworth sees it) is an expression of the existence of God and one which punishes us when we commit immoral acts – like stealing someone else's boat.

We can also see this extract as charting the passage from innocence to experience, from childhood to adulthood. In the first part of the extract Wordsworth is totally in control – of the boat, the situation and his emotions. What he is doing may be wrong but it is clearly enjoyable for a brief period: this can be seen as showing how attractive it is to sin – we are tempted to do wrong because some sins are very attractive and pleasurable. But the sudden appearance of the mountain changes everything and shows the young poet that he is not in control: there is a higher power that watches over us. In simpler terms we might say that the mountain symbolizes his guilty conscience.

Conflict

This extract is remarkable for the power that Nature has over the young Wordsworth. Nature's influence makes him feel guilt for his casual theft of the boat and exerts a moral influence on him lasting for a long time after the incident. The long poem – *The Prelude* (from which this is an extract) – is full of examples of nature's influence on Wordsworth's spiritual and moral development, demonstrating Wordsworth's Pantheism. There is conflict in the poem too: again the conflict centres around the theft of the boat, and it really involves the internal conflict and guilt that Wordsworth feels and which is heightened by Nature and the looming crag that seems to rise up and overpower him. Wordsworth's personification, his animation of Nature greatly aids the impression on the reader.

A Romantic Poem?

This extract is typically Romantic as is the whole of *The Prelude*. The very act of writing a long autobiographical poem about himself suggests that Wordsworth considers himself an exceptional individual with important truths to convey through his poetry. The supreme importance given to nature – in this passage and elsewhere in *The Prelude* – also marks it out as typically romantic, as does Wordsworth's pantheistic notion that Nature is a living force that can inculcate morality.

Why?

This very famous extract:

- shows nature as a moral and spiritual guide.

- explores the psychology of a young boy and his intense feelings of guilt.

- the importance it attaches to Nature make it a typically Romantic poem.

- explores the attractiveness of wrong-doing, but also the effects of a guilty conscience.

- demonstrates a deep love of and respect for nature.

- focuses very closely on the individual and his relationship with nature.

'The Man He Killed' – Thomas Hardy

Author

 Thomas Hardy (1840 – 1928) is best known as a novelist. He wrote 15 novels, most of which are set largely in Dorset and the surrounding counties, and which deal with the ordinary lives of ordinary people in stories in which they struggle to find happiness and love – often battling against fate or their own circumstances. His final two novels *Tess of the D'Urbervilles* (1891) and *Jude the Obscure* (1895) both portray sex outside marriage in a sympathetic way and there was such a hysterical public outcry about the novels that Hardy stopped writing fiction and devoted the rest of his life to poetry. Although some of his poetry is intensely personal, this poem is also typical of his work in that it gives a voice to an ordinary man. Although Hardy trained as an architect, he came from a fairly poor family and, in both his novels and his fiction, he never forgets his roots – often making the rural poor central characters in his novels or giving them a voice in his poetry, as he does here.

Context

Who? The speaker of the poem is an ordinary, working class man who joined the army. The poem is a dramatic monologue.

When? Hardy wrote the poem in 1902 when Britain was fighting the Boers in South Africa in the Second Boer War. The Boers were settlers of Dutch descent who did not want to be subsumed within the British

Empire. British public opinion was divided on the issue of the Boer War – Hardy saw it as the British, motivated by South Africa's gold and diamond mines, meddling in the affairs of independent settlers who were simply trying to defend their homes and did not want to be part of the British Empire. Hardy opposed the war.

Where? There is no indication of where the speaker is (although given the poem itself and its contents, one can imagine the poem being part of an anecdotal pub conversation). The action of the poem takes place on an unnamed battlefield.

What? The speaker of the poem tells an anecdote about a man he killed during a war. The poem is a dramatic monologue, addressed seemingly to an acquaintance of the speaker and attempts to explain why the speaker killed a man in warfare.

inn – pub, public house.

nipperkin – a measure of beer roughly equivalent to a third of a pint and most common in the West Country.

foe – enemy.

'list – enlist in the army.

Off-hand – casually, without serious conviction.

sold his traps – the speaker assumes the man joined the army because he had sold his traps – presumably traps to catch rabbits and other game.

quaint – strange.

half a crown – an old unit of currency.

In the first stanza the speaker admits that the man he killed and he would probably have enjoyed a drink together:

Had he and I but met

By some old ancient inn.

However, as they met in war-time as infantry soldiers "staring face to face", they shot at each other and the speaker "killed him in his place".

In the third stanza the speaker tries to offer an explanation of why he shot the man:

I shot him dead because —

Because he was my foe.

The repetition of "because" suggests that the speaker is uncertain that this is a good enough reason, a point underlined by his statement in the third and fourth lines:

…my foe of course he was;

That's clear enough.

But the next word is "although" as the speaker and former soldier realizes there is some fault in his logic, and then Hardy uses enjambment from the third stanza to the fourth as the man's train of thought continues and he realizes (despite the man being called his "foe"), that the man he killed and he probably had a lot in common: that the man enlisted "Off-hand like — just as I" or perhaps he was simply out of work.

The repetition of "because" also suggests hesitation and a lack of certainty, while the word "foe" (repeated twice) suggests that it is not the man's word: he has been told by propaganda that the men they are fighting are his "foe". The phrase "my foe" is repeated too, which suggests perhaps that he is trying to convince himself of the justice of what he did or that he has heard the word used by a senior officer — both possibilities might be true. Hardy foregrounds the word "foe" not just through repetition but also through the internal rhyme with "so" in line three of the third stanza. The final line of the stanza is "No other reason why" and, although Hardy's speaker is too naïve to follow this thought to its logical conclusion, those simple words – "No other reason why" – explode all the myths about why men fight for their country: honour, glory, a sense of duty, patriotism, loyalty to one's King or Queen, loyalty to one's country or to one's flag. All these are exposed as lies by the simple words of Hardy's ex-soldier. Hardy's speaker cannot articulate these arguments but he does observe in the final stanza "How curious and quaint war is", because it pits men who might have much in common – who, indeed, might have shared a beer together - but calls them the "foe" who must be killed. This is a profoundly anti-war poem.

The other reason war is shown to be less than heroic are the reasons the speaker tells us for joining the army: being out of work or having sold one's traps – "No other reason why" – which completely undercuts all the patriotic reasons for which men supposedly join up.

Hardy chooses to use the ballad stanza in the poem: a simple quatrain with a rhyme scheme of ABAB in each stanza. This ancient, egalitarian form is appropriate to his speaker – and Hardy's language is also appropriately chatty and colloquial: there are no metaphors or similes – Hardy is imitating the voice of a working class soldier.

The structure of the poem is significant. The first stanza opens with a positive tone – the picture of two men perhaps enjoying a beer together at a traditional English inn is a positive one.. The second stanza shatters this by revealing that the speaker killed the man. The third stanza attempts to provide a justification for the killing his "foe", while the fourth speculates that they had "perhaps" some shared reasons for enlisting in the army – such as being out of work. The final stanza ends the poem, but all Hardy's working class soldier can conclude is that war is "quaint and curious". Hardy's use of a relatively inarticulate common soldier is important: the reader can see that war (put in the soldier's terms) is absurd and futile – but these are words his speaker would never use. Therefore, the structure of the poem (we might say) moves from casual and light, to casual and dark – a human being has died. It remains casual because of the speaker's colloquial language and his simple explanation for what he did.

Neither soldier is named nor are the armies they are fighting for identified. It is clear that the speaker is intended to be English, but the poem arguably has a universal feel to it – that it could apply to any war in any century. The dashes in the fourth stanza are important too: they are examples of ellipsis: the words they separate are shortened forms and help to give an impression of a real speaker. However, coming after "perhaps" in the first line of the stanza it is also as though the speaker is hesitantly realizing that he and the man he killed had a lot in common. The poem uses several parallel structures and repetition – "I shot at him as he at me", "face to face" and "off-hand like just as I". The most important parallel structure – that the two men are essentially very similar is implied throughout the poem.

Hardy's use of a working class soldier is absolutely vital to the effect of this poem. Both the speaker and the man he killed have been following orders given to them by their officers from higher classes. If a state of war did not exist, then they would have enjoyed a beer together. And where does the word "foe" come from: it would appear to be a word the soldier has heard from a superior officer or perhaps read in a newspaper – which are so keen to whip up jingoistic sentiment in a time of war.

Conflict

The war the man he killed died in is the obvious conflict in the poem. However, there is another conflict – within the speaker himself. Although he attempts to justify the killing – he was his 'foe' and they were 'ranged as infantry/And staring face to face' – his efforts to do this are rather naïve. The man he killed is still someone with whom he could have enjoyed a few beers. His conclusion – 'How quaint and curious war is' – is naïve because – as we are well aware – wars do not simply happen, politicians decide that they should happen and send men to their deaths. Therefore, because of the speaker's lack of understanding, there is likely to be a conflict between his stated view of war and the readers'.

This short but powerful poem by Hardy:

- uses a working class soldier to expose the futility and absurdity of war.

- shows that the demonization of the enemy as the "foe" is an important device to justify murder.

- demonstrates that the working classes of different countries have more in common than their rulers or those (the government) who choose to go to war.

- demonstrates the dreadful randomness of warfare: the two men were "staring face to face" and one was lucky enough to live.

- uses colloquial language throughout the poem to give a realistic sense of the speaker's voice.

'Cousin Kate' – Christina Rossetti

Author & Context

Christina Rossetti was born in 1830 into a highly talented family – all of whom wrote or painted – and Rossetti was encouraged by her family to pursue her artistic talents from an early age. Her father, a poet and translator, lived in exile, and the family were held together by the mother who had a very strong Christian faith. Rossetti's mother was Francis Polidori, the sister of John Polidori who wrote an early Gothic story called *The Vampyr*. He wrote it while on holiday in 1816 with Percy and Mary Shelley, and Lord Byron. They decided to have a competition to tell the scariest story: it is from this same party game that Mary Shelley's famous novel *Frankenstein* emerged.

Rossetti's poetry revolves around the themes of love and death, and there is often a strong religious dimension to her work. Love in her poems is often presented as problematical – unrequited, unreturned or unfulfilled. As she grew older her work became increasingly religious in tone and subject matter. She also wrote many poems for children.

Her own life was increasingly unhappy: she was engaged to be married twice, but broke off both engagements. She suffered terrible ill-health, although she continued to write, and her final years were darkened by the deaths of most of her family and her two previous lovers. She died in 1894, having achieved much acclaim for her writing. Her brother was Dante Gabriel Rossetti who wrote poetry but who was a painter and member of a group of painters known as the Pre-Raphaelites. The Pre-Raphaelites took much of their inspiration from the Middle Ages and it is possible to see the same tendency in some of Christina Rossetti's work.

maiden – young woman, but with the implication she was a virgin.

flaxen – very blonde.

Woe's me for joy thereof – woe (sadness) to me for the happy time I lived in his palace.

knot – a true lover's knot, often made from thread and worn sometimes as a ring.

mean estate – poor, working class background.

coronet – small crown, which shows that the man is a member of the aristocracy.

fret – worry.

Who? Rossetti adopts the voice of a simple country girl who has been seduced by the lord of the manor and then rejected in favour of her own Cousin – the Cousin Kate of the title. Rossetti also gives us a strong sense of the community looking on and judging these events, though none are named. The poem is a dramatic monologue, spoken by the rejected woman and directly addressed to her rival in love – her cousin Kate.

When? This is a hard question to answer. Of course, it could be contemporary to Rossetti in some remote rural part of the British Isles, but other factors suggest it is located in an unidentified past. The serious points it makes are probably true of all societies at all times – it is still traumatic to have one's love betrayed. However, Rossetti's use of what is essentially the ballad form (as we will see below) gives a timeless atmosphere to the poem.

Where? In a small rural community which is dominated by the lord of the manor's palace.

What? The speaker tells us that she was seduced by the lord of the manor and lived with him in his palace, but did not marry him even though he made her pregnant. Her place is taken by her Cousin Kate who is "pure" (i.e. a virgin) and whom the lord does marry. The speaker's anger and rage at her cousin are only mollified by the fact that Kate does not seem able to conceive and, therefore, cannot give the lord of the manor the thing he most craves – an heir – which ironically the speaker has provided – albeit illegitimately.

Commentary

The earliest surviving ballads in English date from the Middle Ages and are anonymous. They use the ballad stanza – a quatrain with a rhyme scheme of ABCB, but some six line ballads exist (the last two lines often being a repeated refrain) and there are some eight line ballads – formed (as Rossetti's poem is) by combining two quatrains to form an octet. The odd lines have 8 syllables generally; the even lines 6.

Traditional ballads are usually set in an unidentified rural landscape and they always tell a story. The stories that traditional ballads tell are full of the most basic of human emotions –death, betrayal, revenge, and love in all its forms - unrequited, unfulfilled, unreturned, unwanted. The language is usually very simple and the narrative impels the ballad forward. Ballads often used repetition and were originally written to be sung or read aloud. In Rossetti's poem the language is simple (she is adopting the persona and voice of a simple country girl) and all the even lines rhyme. This background is important: Rossetti is writing in a long-established tradition and is, in a sense, writing her own Medieval ballad. She joins two quatrains together to come up with an eight line stanza. It is certainly written in the spirit of the ballad tradition and has an almost timeless quality to it – as though the events of the poem could have taken place at any point over the previous four or five centuries – or even contemporary to Rossetti's writing of the poem.

In the opening stanza the speaker (whose name we never know) tells us the past when she was happy ("Contented with my cottage mates") and unaware that she was an attractive woman ("Not mindful I was fair"). The stanza ends with two rhetorical questions:

Why did a great lord find me out,

And praise my flaxen hair?

Why did a great lord find me out

To fill my heart with care?

Note the simple repetition in lines 5 and 7. The rhetorical questions are full of pain and anguish when we read the rest of the poem: she had been perfectly content before the "great lord" noticed her, but now her "heart is full of care" – for reasons which we can only guess at this point in the poem.

In the second stanza the lord sets her up as his mistress in his palace – a contrast to the poor cottage she has lived in. There she leads a "shameless shameful life": this apparent paradox is simple, I think: her life was "shameless" – she and the great lord enjoyed great physical intimacy and she felt secure in his palace. But she is aware that their relationship is "shameful" because they are not married. The lord's attitude to the speaker is presented as casual: she was his "plaything" and he "changed me like a glove" which suggests his feelings for her are superficial –

So now I moan, an unclean thing,

Who might have been a dove.

She is now considered "unclean" by her community because she is no longer a virgin and has lived a "shameful life" in the lord's palace. The image of the glove shows the ease with which the lord casts her aside and breaks their relationship, while the image of the dove is a traditional symbol of innocence – the person the speaker might have been had she not been seduced by the lord.

The third stanza addresses Kate directly for the first time and by addressing her as "Lady Kate" foreshadows what is about to happen. Cousin Kate grew more beautiful than the speaker, the lord sees her, casts the speak.er aside and marries Kate, thus changing her social class:

He lifted you from mean estate

To sit with him on high.

He is able to get away with such egregious behaviour because of his high social status.

The opening of the fourth stanza shows enormous hypocrisy on the part of the lord and the community:

Because you were so good and pure

He bound you with his ring:

The neighbours call you good and pure,

Call me an outcast thing.

But she is only an "outcast thing" because the lord took her virginity:

the speaker was good and pure once and the fact that she is no longer is purely the lord's doing. The speaker's sadness, trauma and despair are well-captured in the way she sits and howls in dust. The stanza ends with the line, addressed to Kate – "You had the stronger wing": this may refer back to the image of the speaker as a dove, but it also looks forward to the next stanza. Kate with a "stronger wing" is able to fly higher socially.

In the fifth stanza the speaker insists that "my love was true", while she accuses Kate of not really loving the lord – "Your love was writ in sand". The speaker vehemently asserts that – had their positions been reversed and Kate had been his mistress – the speaker would have rejected the lord's offer of marriage: "He'd not have won me with his love". She accuses Kate of having mercenary values and suggests that the lord "bought [Kate] with his land". The bitter vehemence of the speaker is clearly demonstrated in her alleged reaction to the lord, had her and Kate's positions been reversed - "I would have spit into his face". The speaker does not tell us but we might infer she is claiming that she would have shown greater family loyalty than her Cousin Kate has done. She also alleges that Kate is only interested in the lord's land and the social position that goes with it.

The final stanza is the climax of the poem and the zenith of the speaker's revengeful feelings. The stanza opens cryptically – "Yet I've a gift you have not got". Kate may have many fine "clothes and [a] wedding ring". But the speaker has a "fair-haired son" while the lord and Kate remain childless. The speaker's description of her son as "my shame" and "my pride" makes perfect sense: he is her shame because he is evidence that she had sex outside marriage with the lord is now treated as an outcast by her community; and he is her pride because she is full of maternal love for him.

Rossetti uses structure cleverly. We know by line 11 that the narrator is moaning and thinks of herself as an "unclean thing", but Cousin Kate's part in all this is delayed until stanza three. The final twist or reveal –

that the speaker has a son by the lord and that Cousin Kate is childless – is left to the final stanza. The speaker has her perfect revenge for her betrayal and the terrible feelings she has suffered.

There is a strong sense of injustice in this poem – or rather Rossetti presents the speaker as having a strong sense of injustice – directed at the lord and at her cousin Kate. As readers, however, we can see that there is a wider injustice at work: both women are very passive and both, in a sense, are victims of a patriarchal society where men take what they want with little thought of the human consequences.

Conflict

There is a bitter conflict between the narrator on the one hand and the Lord and the speaker's Cousin Kate. On the surface, this is to do with love – the Lord's betrayal of the narrator and his choice of her cousin Kate to be his wife. However, there is further conflict caused by gender inequality and by class inequality – all the way through the poem we are reminded that the narrator comes from a cottage while the lord lives in his palace home.

.Why?

This bitter ballad by Rossetti:

- demonstrates the anger and rage that can arise from rejection of love and the failure of relationships;

- reveals the gender inequality at the heart of the society it describes;

- shows the sexual hypocrisy in society over the different attitudes to male and female sexuality;

- shows the deference of ordinary people towards their so-called social betters;

- shows the importance and malign influence of class in society;

- seethes with a desire for revenge on the part of the speaker. The final stanza is redolent with schadenfreude (the pleasure you take in someone else's misfortune – here the inability of the lord and his wife to have children).

'Exposure' – Wilfred Owen

Context

 Wilfred Owen (1893 – 1918) is widely regarded as the leading British poet of the First World War. He died in action on November 4th 1918 – just seven days before the war finally came to an end. Owen was an officer and was awarded the Military Cross for leadership and bravery in October 1918. The shock of what he saw in the front-line moved him to produce a great many poems in a very short time – most of which were not published until after his death. He seems to have been particularly keen to ensure that the British public was told the horrific truth about the war. He developed his own use of half-rhyme which was to influence other poets for the whole of the 20th century. Owen famously wrote that his subject was not war, but the pity of war – a feeling that is especially apparent in this poem. "Above all I am not concerned with Poetry. My subject is War, and the pity of War. The Poetry is in the pity."

It is over a hundred years since the First World War began, and, because of the many commemorations, many readers will have a visual sense of what that war was like. In fact, it was a world war with fighting taking place on almost every continent, but the abiding memory of the war – a memory based on photos, documentaries and even poems like this one, is of the trench warfare on the Western Front in Belgium and France. There are clear reasons for this. The war waged in the trenches resulted in battles with enormous loss of life with very little ground gained: on the first day of the Battle of the Somme the British army suffered 70,000 casualties, 20,000 of whom were killed. I think the other reason the Western Front holds such an important place in our image of the First World War is the trenches themselves and trench life: hundreds of thousands of soldiers living very close to each other in holes in the ground and suffering terrible, barbaric conditions, plagued by rats, lice and the cold. So the futility and loss of life in the battles, as well as the appalling conditions make the war in the trenches especially memorable.

Who? Owen uses the third person plural – we – to speak on behalf of British soldiers fighting in trenches on the Western Front during the First World War.

When? Not specified, but in the depths of winter during the First World War.

Where? In the trenches of the Western Front. The First World War was a very static war: the trench systems of the Allies and of the Germans stretched from the coast of Belgium to the French border with Switzerland.

What? Owen describes a typical night and the following day in the trenches. The main enemy is not the Germans but the weather; the main feelings not fear or misgivings, but boredom and pointlessness. Owen reflects on why he and his colleagues are there and what they are fighting for.

salient – a one-way trench dug out into No Man's Land to get closer to the enemy

melancholy – dejection, depression

glozed – decorated with

crickets – house crickets: insects which live near or behind old fireplaces and make a distinctive and rhythmic clicking sound

not loath – not unwilling

Throughout the poem Owen speaks for all the soldiers on the Western

Front by using "we" as they face an onslaught from – not the Germans – but the weather. The first stanza starts with a simple, straightforward statement: "Our brains ache in the merciless iced east winds that knive us" – the long vowels of the opening three words suggesting tiredness followed by sibilance and assonance on shorter vowels describing the wind, and ending with "knive us" which turns the wind into a stabbing knife, cutting into them. In the next line, although they cannot sleep, paradoxically it is because the night is silent and they anticipate an attack. They have confused memories of being in a salient and the only light comes from "low, drooping flares"; the sentries are "worried by silence… curious, nervous." But, as Owen tells us in the last line "nothing happens" – words which are repeated four times in the poem.

Owen establishes in the first verse the structure he will use for all eight stanzas of the poem: a five line stanza with the first line half-rhyming with the fourth, and the second and third line rhyming with each other. Half-rhyme (because it sounds wrong - to put it simply) is an apt choice for a poem in which the poet describes a situation where many things are wrong. Very often the rhyme words are trochees as well as being half-rhyme (*nervous / knive us*) and this falling rhythm and the feminine endings to the lines intensify the sense of anti-climax and a poignant sort of futility. It also – along with the final shortened line produces a strange sense of apathy. The fifth and final line of each verse is much shorter than the others and acts as an anti-climax: again this is highly appropriate, because, despite all the nervous anticipation, this is a poem in which nothing happens. The fact that the fourth line rhymes with the first is important too: by the time the reader reaches the fourth line we are directed back to the first line by the half-rhyme. The stanza looks inward so to speak and this is appropriate in a poem which describes a stalemate and which is concerned largely with the inner thoughts and feelings of the soldiers.

The first word of the second stanza – "Watching" – suggests the soldiers' passivity: they have nothing to do except wait, but their senses are keenly attuned to their surroundings and the possibility of attack.

They hear the "mad gusts tugging on the [barbed] wire" which only serves to remind them of the "twitching agonies" of men caught and dying on the wire. From the north "the flickering gunnery rumbles" – a striking image which combines an image of light with onomatopoeia and is given aural cohesion by the assonance in "gunnery rumbles", assonance which is continued in the next line with "dull rumour". The stanza ends with the poignant question: "What are we doing here?"

In the third stanza dawn comes but it brings no respite, no hope. The soldiers give the impression of being reduced to survival of the elements: "We only know war lasts, rain soaks, and clouds sag stormy" Owen then introduces a metaphor related to the war to describe the heavy rain clouds that are heading their way:

Dawn massing in the east her melancholy army

Attacks once more in ranks on shivering ranks of grey.

The German army wore grey uniforms which makes the personification even more apposite, but only rain faces the soldiers. And once again "Nothing happens."

The fourth stanza begins with a superbly written line, the sibilance of 's' giving an aural impression of the sound of gunfire. But it is not threatening and Owen remarks that the bullets are "less deadly than the air that shudders black with snow". The next line alliterates on 'f' to describe the gentle snowflakes and the caesuras and verbs – "flock, pause and renew" attempt to suggest the swirling, random movement of the snowflakes. The soldiers are reduced to passivity again – watching the snowflakes. "But still nothing happens".

The next stanza shows how exposed the British soldiers were to the elements: it's as if the snowflakes are deliberately seeking them out:

Pale flakes with lingering stealth come feeling for our faces.

And here the personification and the "stealth" make the snowflakes appear especially malevolent. The personification of the snowflakes and the phrase "come feeling for our faces" suggests a curiously evil intimacy. As the soldiers "cringe in holes" their minds reminisce about happier times – of "grassier ditches" and "blossoms trickling where the blackbird fusses". But the stanza ends on an ominous note as Owen asks "Is it that we are dying?" The uncertainty engendered by the question is deliberately unnerving.

The sixth stanza is a respite from the weather. "Slowly our ghosts drag home" and the soldiers think about their homes, but the thought brings little joy as the house belongs to the crickets and the mice:

> *The house is theirs;*

> *Shutter and doors are closed: on us the doors are closed –*

> *We turn back to our dying.*

The seventh stanza appears to offer a justification for the war. If we follow the sense from the previous stanza:

> *We turn back to our dying.*

> *Since we believe not otherwise can kind fires burn;*

> *Nor ever suns smile true on child, or field, or fruit.*

These lines imply that the soldiers are there to ensure that "kind fires can burn" and that because of their participation in the war suns will smile true on "child, or field, or fruit". Paradoxically their love is made afraid of "God's invincible spring" which suggests that they believe that God is on their side, Winter will be displaced by Spring and – ironically – the better weather will allow real fighting to begin – which is why they are afraid. But, conscious that they are defending a just cause, "we lie out here; therefore were born" – which suggests that what they are doing is both their destiny and their duty. However, Owen's faith in the Christian God is given a tentative rebuke when he writes "but love of God seems dying" – how could God allow such horrendous suffering on such a colossal scale?

But despite this stanza of justification, Owen in the final stanza returns to the grim reality of winter in the trenches:

Tonight, His frost will fasten on this mud and us,

Shrivelling many hands and puckering foreheads crisp.

"His frost" is God's frost; there seems little evidence of God's love for suffering humanity in this poem: during the night some men will die of hypothermia, to be buried on the next day:

The burying party, picks and shovels in their shaking grasp,

Pause over half-known faces. All their eyes are ice.

But nothing happens.

Owen has succeeded in writing a poem which details in excruciating detail the desperate conditions endured in winter in the trenches, where the main enemy was not the German Army but the atrocious winter weather – men literally froze to death. He also conveys a sense of the sheer boredom of waiting for something, anything, to happen and questions repeatedly what the soldiers are doing there. He also includes two verses which allow the men to think about their homes and offers a justification for their being there – to allow kind fires to burn.

"Exposure" is not one of Owen's best-known poems, but perhaps it deserves to be: the use of half-rhyme, the stanza structure that turns in upon itself, and the truncated last line are wholly appropriate to the subject matter of the poem – the soldiers' doubts about why they are there and their doubt about God's role in their suffering. I find the last short line of each stanza especially effective since it leads nowhere – just as the men are going nowhere and seem to have lost all purpose.

Conflict

The central conflict in 'Exposure' is between the atrocious weather conditions and the British soldiers defenceless against the rain, the snow and the frost. In the final verse some men have frozen to death overnight. The war is irrelevant in this poem. Another source of conflict is the sheer boredom the soldiers experience, waiting for something to happen and the doubts they have about why they are there – doing nothing except battling the atrocious weather conditions. Stanza six shows the conflict between the men's memories of home and their current experiences. While stanza seven introduces conflict with God and his part in all this: after all, in the following stanza it is "His frost" (the capitalization is all important) which kills the men in the night.

In terms of power the winter weather seems all powerful, but, despite the toll taken by the winter, the soldiers show a hardy resilience and Owen's very act of writing the poem shows a certain triumph of art over horrendous living conditions.

Why?

This long poem:

- gives us a vivid picture of life in the trenches in winter;

- makes clear the boredom and the lack of action that the soldiers had to endure;

- shows the horrendous, life-threatening weather conditions in the trenches;

- expresses nostalgia for their homes;

- questions both God's part in the war and the very reason the men are fighting.

'The Charge of the Light Brigade' – Alfred, Lord Tennyson

Context

Alfred Tennyson was born in 1809 and died in 1892. His early work received a mixed reaction, but his *Poems* published in 1842 established him as the leading poet of his day. In 1850 he was made Poet Laureate and was given a peerage in 1884. This poem is not especially typical of his work. It was published in 1855 in a collection called *Maud* and was written in response to a British military disaster during the Battle of Balaklava in October 1854. It is said that Tennyson read the report of the disaster in *The Times* and was moved to write the poem.

The Crimean War was fought largely in the Crimean Peninsula – then part of the Russian Empire and was until recently part of the Ukraine before the Crimean Peninsula was annexed by Russia in 2014. Britain and its allies – France and the Ottoman Empire – were fighting Russia over who would control the Dardenelles – the narrow strip of sea in Turkey that connects the Aegean Sea to the Black Sea. It was important for British sea-routes and trade that Russia did not control the Dardenelles, but it was important for Russia as it gave her access to the Mediterranean.

This is the report from *The Times* that Tennyson read:

At ten past eleven our Light Cavalry Brigade rushed to the front....The whole brigade scarcely made one effective regiment, according to the numbers of continental armies; and yet it was more than we could spare. As they passed towards the front, the Russians opened on them from the guns in the redoubts on the right, with volleys of musketry and rifles.

They swept proudly past, glittering in the morning sun in all the pride and splendour of war. We could hardly believe the evidence of our senses! Surely that handful of men were not going to charge an army in position? Alas! it was too true – their desperate valour knew no bounds, and far indeed was it removed from its so called better part – discretion. They advanced in two lines, quickening their pace as they closed towards the enemy. A more fearful spectacle was never witnessed than by those who, without the power to aid, beheld their heroic countrymen rushing to the arms of death. At the distance of 1200 yards the whole line of the enemy belched forth, from thirty iron mouths, a flood of smoke and flame, through which hissed the deadly balls. Their flight was marked by instant gaps in our ranks, by dead men and horses, by steeds flying wounded or riderless across the plain. The first line was broken – it was joined by the second, they never halted or checked their speed an instant. With diminished ranks, thinned by those thirty guns, which the Russians had laid with the most deadly accuracy, with a halo of flashing steel above their heads, and with a cheer which was many a noble fellow's death cry, they flew into the smoke of the batteries; but ere they were lost from view, the plain was strewed with their bodies and with the carcasses of horses. They were exposed to an oblique fire from the batteries on the hills on both sides, as well as to a direct fire of musketry.

Through the clouds of smoke we could see their sabres flashing as they rode up to the guns and dashed between them, cutting down the gunners as they stood. The blaze of their steel, as an officer standing near me said, was 'like the turn of a shoal of mackerel'. We saw them riding through the guns, as I have said; to our delight we saw them returning, after breaking through a column of Russian infantry, and scattering them like chaff, when the flank fire of the battery on the hill swept them down, scattered and broken as they were. Wounded men and dismounted troopers flying towards us told the sad tale – demigods could not have done what they had failed to do.

At the very moment when they were about to retreat, an enormous mass of lancers was hurled upon their flank…With courage too great almost for credence, they were breaking their way through the columns which enveloped them, when there took place an act of atrocity without parallel in the modern warfare of civilized nations. The Russian gunners, when the storm of cavalry passed, returned to their guns. They saw their own cavalry mingled with the troopers who had just ridden over them, and to the eternal disgrace of the Russian name the miscreants poured *a murderous volley of grape and canister on the mass of struggling men and horses, mingling friend and foe in one common ruin…At twenty five to twelve not a British soldier, except the dead and dying, was left in front of these bloody Muscovite guns.*

And this is what *The Times* editorial said about the disaster:

Causeless and fruitless, it stands by itself as a grand heroic deed, surpassing even that spectacle of a shipwrecked regiment, setting down into the waves, each man still in his rank. The British soldier will do his duty, even to certain death, and is not paralyzed by feeling that he is the victim of **some hideous blunder.** [My emboldening.]

Why have I bothered to reprint this article? I think it is important for you to see the inspiration that Tennyson used. He had not been to the Crimea; he had never been on a battlefield; his only source was this article. *Some hideous blunder* is directly reflected in line 12 of the poem. Equally the reporter's assertion that the British soldier will *do his duty, even to certain death is* the main theme of the poem. The Light Brigade began the charge with 607 men; only 302 returned. I think *The Times* report is interesting – not simply because it is a first-hand account by a journalist who witnessed the event. The editorial admits there was *some hideous blunder*, but the overwhelming tone of the report and the editorial is admiration for the courage of the men who obeyed such a senseless order. We can see in Tennyson's poem a similar balance: he does admit it was a terrible mistake, but his emphasis is on the heroism of the men who simply obeyed their orders.

In reality, the incident was a complete failure and a pointless loss of life – it was a military disaster. However, it has become famous, partly through Tennyson's poem, but also because it moved other artists to produce work based on the incident. Perhaps it appealed to something that the public wanted to believe was part of being British – unflinching courage against the odds. Over the course of time, Tennyson's poem has lost some of its popularity perhaps because our attitudes to war have changed and we are more likely to question the justness of any war and the human cost of blindly following orders. In

Tennyson's defence, one might say that as Poet Laureate it was his task to reflect the national mood at the time and it is certainly true that the men who charged on that day did display great courage.

league – three miles.

Valley of Death – an allusion to Psalm 23 in the Bible and to a novel called *Pilgrim's Progress* by John Bunyan. In both texts faith in God encourages people to be brave in dangerous places.

Light Brigade – at school I was confused about this title. It means that the brigade were on horseback but were lightly armed – they only carried swords. And, yes – there was a Heavy Brigade who moved more slowly because they carried more weaponry.

sabres – the specific type of sword carried by the soldiers.

Cossack – an ethnic group from south-eastern Russia, famed for their fighting skills and bravery.

sunder'd – broken apart.

Back from the mouth of Hell – anthropologists have noted that in cultures all over the world there are stories about brave men who visit hell or the underworld or the world of the dead and return alive. For example, in Greek mythology Hercules visits the underworld, but returns unscathed, adding to his heroic qualities. Tennyson is deliberately adding the members of the Light Brigade to this long and brave tradition.

Who? Tennyson writes about the cavalrymen of the Light Brigade; the enemy is present in the poem, as is the person who gave the order to charge the Russian guns; the reader is addressed directly in the final stanza.

When? October 25th, 1854, although Tennyson wrote the poem a few days later having read the report in *The Times*.

Where? Outside the Russian town of Balaklava in the Crimean Peninsula.

What? Tennyson describes the charge of the cavalry and what happened to them.

Commentary

This very famous poem relies a great deal on repetition throughout its length. Tennyson also uses alliteration in many lines and, if you read it aloud, the rhythm of the poem seems to imitate the motion of the horses galloping forward. It is these features, I would suggest, which make the poem so memorable.

The opening stanza highlights the order the brigade was given in lines 5 and 6. The opening phrase is repeated three times; *Valley of Death* is repeated twice as is *the six hundred* – giving these phrases prominence and emphasizing that they are going to die and their relatively small numbers. The phrase *Valley of Death* would have been very evocative to a Christian audience because it comes from such a well-known psalm.

The second stanza is directly related to the report in *The Times*. Line 9 repeats line 5. Line 12 picks up the word used by the journalist, but makes the order anonymous – *Someone had blunder'd*. It is not part of Tennyson's aim to apportion blame for the order, but to praise the men who followed it. And it is important, in the poem, that the soldiers knew it was a blunder yet still went ahead and charged: it shows their blind obedience to orders and their bravery. Lines 13 to 15 use repetition but also heap praise on their unquestioning obedience of the order, despite having a clear understanding that it would lead to death. The alliteration in line 15 – *do and die* – draws attention their clear courage and willingness to die.

In stanza three Tennyson makes us aware of the enemy again, through simple repetition which here gives us a real sense of the situation into which they rode, facing cannon fire from three sides. Note the onomatopoeia of *thunder'd* and the alliteration in line 22. In lines 24 and 25 Tennyson uses synonyms for the Valley of Death – *the jaws of Death* and *the mouth of Hell*. Although he concentrates on their bravery, line 23 also mentions their skill. They rode *well* and *boldly*, despite the terrible situation they were in.

Stanza four describes what happened when the cavalry reached the Russian positions. Tennyson uses vivid verbs – *flash'd, charging, plunged* – to give us an impression of close quarter fighting. *Charging an army* reminds us of the impossible odds they faced, while *All the world wonder'd* might mean that the world looks on amazed at their courage or astonished at the stupidity of the order – it probably means both! They have some limited success when in close contact with the enemy: the Russians *reel'd* and were *shatter'd and sunder'd*. Finally at the end of the stanza they turn to ride back to the British positions – those that are left. Note Tennyson's repeated use of the phrase *the six hundred*, except that it is now preceded by *not*.

The brigade ride back to their own positions in stanza five. Again Tennyson repeats several lines and phrases from earlier in the poem. The first three lines are identical to the start of stanza three with only one word being altered. He uses more alliteration in line 44 and pays tribute to the soldiers with the word *hero* and by pointing out that they had fought so well.

The sixth stanza is short and directly addressed to the reader. It begins with a question which stresses their glory (and not the idiocy of the order); the second line is an exclamation of admiration and is followed by a line we have seen before which suggests their charge will become famous all over the world. The final three lines are imperatives, orders to the readers – we are told to honour the Light Brigade because they were so noble.

How attitudes have changed since 1854! Today if so many British soldiers died in one engagement that lasted only half an hour, there would be a public outcry and calls for an enquiry – particularly if it emerged that they died because of an incompetent order or an order that was misinterpreted. But Tennyson is not interested in that side of this story and in the past such an inquiry is much less likely to have occurred. He wants to praise their unthinking bravery and willingness to die following orders. You may find it hard to agree with the attitudes in the poem, but there is no doubt that Tennyson uses all his poetic skills to create something memorable.

Conflict

The questions of conflict and power are very ambivalent in this poem. Despite their appalling losses and the fact that this attack was a terrible failure, Tennyson manages to suggest the power of the Light Brigade's charge through his use of anapaests, coupled with the occasional trochee at the start of some lines. It is this which helps to make the charge sound heroic and brave. Of course, the Russian artillery are a major source of conflict and, throughout the charge, the Russians hold all the real power. More widely, the poem is about a wider conflict – the Crimean War. There is further conflict on the British side which Tennyson acknowledges: the ill-judged order for the Light Brigade to charge ("someone had blundered"), yet it is a tribute to the self-discipline of the Brigade that they obey the order. The power of discipline in the British Army is a quality which Tennyson's poem recognizes and celebrates, despite the disastrous result. Yet the real power in the poem is that of the Russian cannon which caused such heavy losses on the Light Brigade. The ultimate conflict in the poem is the unwavering courage of the members of the Light Brigade who obeyed without question an order which sent many of them to certain death and whether it was right for them to do so. I think the modern reader might feel some conflict when reading Tennyson's poem, because he does glamourize war and its participants and our modern attitudes to war and its victims is very different, because of the enormous suffering in two world wars and countless minor conflicts.

Why?

This very well-known and famous poem

- gives a vivid impression of the speed of the charge and the atmosphere of battle.

- glorifies the courage and heroism of the men who followed orders and made the charge.

- tells us to remember the dead and their noble deeds.

- is unashamedly patriotic and celebratory of the courage shown by the soldiers.

'Half-caste' – John Agard

Author & Context

John Agard was born in the former British colony of Guyana in 1949 and he has written many books for children and adults. He moved to Britain in 1977 and lives in Sussex with his partner Grace Nichols – who is also a poet. Agard is well-known as a skilled and adept performer of his own poems and you may get the chance to see him perform his poems during your course. You should check out his performance of the poem 'Half-Caste' on YouTube, because his performance helps to bring the poem alive. In many of his poems he uses Caribbean accent and dialect to bring a Guyanese identity to his work, but he also uses Standard English in some poems.

'Half-caste' is a term for a category of people of mixed race or ethnicity. It is derived from the term *caste*, which comes from the Latin *castus*, meaning pure, and the derivative Portuguese and Spanish *casta*, meaning race, and is generally considered offensive. Because of its derivation from the Latin, 'half-caste' implies someone who is half-pure or impure: it is for this reason that the term 'mixed race' is considered more accurate and acceptable.

yuself – yourself

yu - you

Picasso – a very famous 20th century painter

dat – that

some of dem cloud – some of those clouds

de – the

ah rass – oh shit

Tchaikovsky – a famous 19th century Russian composer dah - the

an – and

wha - what

ah – I

wud – would

mih - my

Who? Although Agard addresses 'yu', the poem's message is directed at all those who use the term half-caste.

When? In modern Britain.

Where? In the United Kingdom.

What? In a deeply serious poem, Agard uses humour to mock and ridicule the term half-caste.

This poem deals with a very serious issue and one that the poet cares deeply about, but does so at times in a funny way in order to mock those the poem is protesting about and attacking. Agard is angry at the use of the term 'half-caste' and uses mockery and ridicule to challenge the term, but the poem can be seen as hostile to any form of racial prejudice or judging anyone on the colour of their skin. This poem is also written to be performed so that the opening short verse:

Excuse me

standing on one leg

I'm half-caste.

would be visually funny as the poet mimics the words and starts the performance of the poem on one leg. Throughout the poem Agard chooses his words very carefully, so that he writes words which are a mixture of standard, 'correct' English and words which come from Black British patois or are phonetically spelt (spelt to mimic the way they are said). Therefore, even in his language Agard mirrors the theme of the poem – which is all about mixing – by deliberately mixing patois with standard English. For most of the poem Agard rejects traditional punctuation to show that he does not need to conform to convention or to show his rebellion at convention.

After the first verse the poem's speaker asks for an explanation of half-caste and asks a series of ridiculous rhetorical questions which serve to highlight the stupidity of the term. He asks whether Picasso when he mixed 'red and green' produced a 'half-caste canvas' and whether on a day of sunshine and clouds, light and dark, we speak of 'half-caste weather'. It is white English people who use the term and Agard jokily points out that most English weather

nearly always half-caste

in fact some of dem cloud

half-caste til dem overcast

so spiteful dem don't want de sun to pass

'Spiteful' here is clearly referring to the clouds but it is easy, by extension, to see it as referring to the sort of people who unthinkingly and insensitively use the term 'half-caste' to describe people. He goes on to ask whether Tchaikovsky's symphonies should be called 'a half-caste symphony' because he used both the black and the white keys of the piano to compose them. The poet demonstrates his own cultured background by mentioning Picasso and Tchaikovsky – two giants of European culture.

The third verse paragraph changes direction. Agard still demands that the user of the term 'half-caste' should explain himself. These lines explore the effect of the term 'half-caste' on the speaker. He says he is only listening to him with half of his ear and looking with only half of his eye; and he only offers half of his hand by way of greeting. These are silly, ridiculous notions – but Agard uses them to attack the use of the term half-caste to show that he cannot engage fully with those who use that term and who show racial prejudice. The whole rhythm of his life is upset – when he sleeps he 'close half-a-eye' and is only able to 'dream half-a-dream'. The use of the term, he claims, stops him from being a full human being – 'I half-caste human being' – in a society which calls him half-caste and which exhibits prejudice based on the colour of people's skin, he is not fully human. Indeed, one might argue that racists are what they are because they refuse to see the common humanity they share with people of all races.

The tone changes in the final few lines. Agard has moved from humour through anger at being rejected to a quiet determination and he asks the other person to come back tomorrow with his complete humanity

Wid de whole of your eye

an de whole of your ear

and de whole of your mind.

an I will tell yu

ae other half

of my story.

If people approach him with their full human consciousness and the right mind-set, they will accept him for what he is and understand that the term 'half-caste' reflects essentially racist attitudes – which is why 'mixed race' is less offensive and more accurate.

The poem is written in free verse – again like the lack of punctuation showing the poet's disregard for traditional convention. But the rhetorical questions and the anaphora – especially the number of times 'half-caste' is used – give the poem cohesion. Structure is also provided by the development of the thoughts of the poet and the final challenge to 'come back tomorrow'.

Conflict

The conflict in this poem is fairly straightforward. Put at its simplest it is between people who are mixed race and those who use the insensitive term 'half-caste' to describe them. More widely, it is a poem about racial prejudice, between those who judge others by the colour of their skin and those who don't.

'Half-caste' by John Agard

- uses humour and ridicule to mock the term 'half-caste';

- ridicules racial prejudice in general

- is a poem of protest about the way mixed race people are treated

- highlights a serious social problem – racism.

'Catrin' – Gillian Clarke

Context

Gillian Clarke who was born in 1937 in Cardiff is one of the leading poets of our time and is very much associated with Wales, where she has lived for most of her life. She and her husband live on a smallholding and keep sheep. Many of her poems are rooted in nature and she is highly aware of environmental issues. You can find a lot of very useful material for students on her website, including comments on most of her poems. Her writing is deeply rooted in everyday experience – sometimes as in this poem personal experience – but also touches on wider, deeper themes. Her poetry is widely studied in schools and she gives regular poetry readings and lectures about poetry.

the tight/Red rope of love – the umbilical cord joining mother to baby

that old red rope – Gillian Clarke has said of this 'The invisible umbilical cord that ties parents and children even when children are grown up. I was also thinking of a boat tied to a harbour wall. The rope is hidden. The boat looks as if it is free, but it isn't.'

Who? The poet addresses her daughter, Catrin, directly.

When? Although the poem starts with Catrin's birth, the final stanza is written when she has grown older and, crucially, more independent.

Where? The first two stanzas are set in the delivery room and the hospital where Catrin was born, but the rest of the poem is set, if anywhere, in the family home.

What? As Gillian Clarke herself once said in an interview 'Catrin' answers the question: 'Why did my beautiful baby have to become a teenager?' The first stanza shows Catrin's complete dependence on her mother as a baby being born; the second stanza shows the desire for independence and freedom that many teenagers feel. It is an intensely personal poem that confronts the physical strain of childbirth and later the tensions that can arise in any parent/child relationship.

Commentary

The first stanza is written looking back at the memory of giving birth. The poet says 'I can remember you – a statement repeated in line 6 as if to emphasize the clarity and strength of the memory. In the opening sentence the poet is simply waiting for the process of child-birth to begin and has time to watch 'The people and cars taking/Turn at the traffic light'. Childbirth can be a very painful and traumatic experience for the mother and the poet describes the act of childbirth as 'our first/Fierce confrontation' fighting over 'the tight red rope of love' – alliteration helps give these lines aural cohesion but more importantly is the idea of childbirth as a fight and a fight that is fierce. The 'tight red rope of love' is a strikingly original phrase and seems as if it should be an oxymoron – we certainly do not associate 'love' with tight ropes or it may remind us of tug of war – one which the baby is bound to lose if it is to survive. The delivery room

... was square

Environmental blank, disinfected

Of paintings or toys

The paintings and toys which will become such a feature of any child's life as it grows and develops, or which await the new-born baby in the family home. The pain of childbirth can cause women to shout and scream, and Clarke uses a metaphor of writing to describe the way she screamed:

I wrote

All over the walls with my

Words, coloured the clean squares

With the wild, tender circles

Of our struggle to become

Separate.

The circles are 'wild' because of the pain, but tender too because she is dealing with a new-born child. The scribbled 'circles' may be a foretaste of Catrin in a few months' time and her first attempts with a crayon or they may be a hint that the mother's language became colourful (i.e. taboo) during the pain of childbirth. Notice how the poet positions the word 'separate' on its own at the beginning of a line – separate from the rest of the sentence. The 'environmental blank' of the delivery room has been coloured in by the shouts and cries and yells of childbirth, and the overwhelming joy and elation that a new healthy baby can produce in its parents. Clarke must have felt such an extreme mixture of emotions – 'wild' and 'tender' in their intensity

The first stanza ends:

We want, we shouted,

To be separate.

As the baby is born 'I' changes to 'we' and the new-born baby's crying is added to the noises in the delivery room. Although bound by the 'tight, red rope of love', the baby must be born and the umbilical cord must be cut.

The second stanza begins by reflecting of the poet and her daughter that 'neither won nor lost the struggle' of childbirth – they both simply survived it. But the poet claims she is still 'fighting [you] off'. Catrin is presented as strong and this is shown in the slowing down of the language and the three adjectives used to describe her hair – 'your straight, long/Brown hair' and her 'glare' which is 'defiant'. It turns out that mother and daughter are arguing about whether the daughter should be allowed to skate outside in the dark for one more hour.

More importantly, they are still (in Clarke's consciousness at least)

joined by 'that old rope' – once the umbilical cord, now the indissoluble ties between mother and daughter. In the poem Catrin's 'defiant glare' brings up, Clarke writes

From the heart's pool that old rope,

Tightening about my life.

Trailing love and conflict.

All this comes from Catrin's glare and, now she is older, Clarke's heart is torn between two extremes – 'love and conflict' – just as in the delivery room the emotions were of pain and physical strain but also the deeply psychological.

Linguistically the two verse paragraphs contrast with each other: the 'dark' of the night contrasts with the brightly-lit delivery room; the 'wild... circles' are contrasted with Catrin's straight, strong, long/Brown hair'; the delivery room was 'hot' in the first stanza, but we might infer that in the second stanza Catrin's face is 'rosy' because she has come indoors after going skating outside – an activity she wants to continue. But both stanzas contain struggle – the first struggle to give birth or to be born which is then contrasted with the mother's struggle to control her child and the child's struggle to get her own way. The dark is, of course, the darkness outside which Catrin wants to go skating in, but it may also symbolize the future – the future of the mother and daughter relationship or Catrin's own individual future, both of which are unknowable.

The poem does not rhyme and has no regular pattern, although most lines have three stressed syllables. There is some internal rhyme. Clarke uses enjambment throughout and this, and the very simple language she uses, gives the impression of a natural speaking voice – which is appropriate in a poem addressed to your daughter.

The poem's tone shifts remarkably too, beginning with the calm and relaxed description of the poet simply watching people and cars waiting for the traffic lights to change, but, as the process of childbirth arrives, the poem, while still descriptive, becomes fraught with tension and pain. The second verse paragraph, although containing some description of Catrin, is also more reflective about their relationship and the tone, although rueful in the face of her daughter's defiance of maternal authority, we should also note the celebratory nature of the poem – Clarke is proud of her daughter and the very close relationship that they have. In the poem Clarke is torn between love for her daughter and care for her well-being – which is what causes the conflict. The old rope that joins them will last a lifetime and bring more conflict underpinned by love.

'Catrin' is an easy poem to relate to: all children as they grow up come into conflict with their parents or carers; many of us will also be parents.

Conflict

The 'struggle' of the first stanza becomes the 'fighting' of the second stanza and the conflict between mother and daughter is described vividly and intensely. There is also conflict within the poet herself: when faced with Catrin's 'defiant glare' at being told she cannot skate outdoors in the dark for another hour, we are told that the glare brings up

From the heart's pool that old rope,

Tightening about my life,

Trailing love and conflict.

Clarke's memory of giving birth to Catrin is still so intense and so paradoxical (the pain of childbirth, the joy at new life) that she is torn between what she calls 'love and conflict'.

Why?

In this poem which uses very simple vocabulary to describe a situation which must face every mother and her children, Clarke:

- vividly suggests the pain and suffering of the mother during childbirth, but also celebrates the strength and personality of her daughter; ..

- shows that the connection between mother and daughter, which started in the heat and trauma of the delivery room, will never fade;

- suggests that just as childbirth brings joy and feelings of tenderness, there will come a time when mother and daughter (despite their love for each other) will have confrontations as the child strives for independence.

'War Photographer' – Carol Ann Duffy

Context

Carol Ann Duffy is one of the UK's most successful and best-known living poets. Her poems have a very wide appeal. On May 1st 2009 she became the nation's Poet Laureate – the first woman ever to hold the position. Her poems are often set for study by the examination boards – because they are thought of very highly and because many of them are very accessible. Her poems often use very modern and everyday language, but in fresh, funny and witty ways. She uses traditional forms like the sonnet and the dramatic monologue, but succeeds in breathing new life into these old forms by the modernity of her writing and subject matter. The accessibility of many of her poems may obscure the fact that she is highly skilled at a very intricate and ingenious manipulation of language.

Carol Ann Duffy was born in 1955 in Glasgow, but grew up in Staffordshire and studied at Liverpool University. Don McCullin was a famous photographer whose images from war-torn countries were widely published and admired. Duffy became friends with McCullin and based this poem on conversations she had with him. "War Photographer" was published in the collection *Standing Female Nude*, which appeared in 1985.

Who? The poem is a third person description of a war photographer (as the title makes clear), but other people are mentioned – the people he has photographed in war-torn countries, the editor of the newspaper he works for, the readers of the Sunday newspapers in which his images will appear.

When? In the late 20th century but before the use of digital cameras and the rise of social media: the photographer develops his own images in his own darkroom.

Where? The action of the poem, recounted by Duffy in the present tense, takes place in England, but the countries the photographer has visited are evoked through his memories of the suffering he has seen.

What? The photographer develops his photographs in his dark room. As the images emerge, he recalls the real life incidents that the photographs are records of. In the final stanza the photographer is flying back to some war-torn country and looks down reflectively on the United Kingdom that he is leaving behind.

Belfast – during the period known as the Troubles, Belfast was the scene of bombings, and murders carried out by all sides in the conflict: the Provisional IRA, the Loyalist paramilitaries and the British Army.

Beirut – the capital of Lebanon and in the 70s and 80s the back-drop to a bloody civil war, sectarian violence between Christian and Islamic militias, and incursions by the Israeli Defence Force to nullify the effect of terrorist attacks on Israel. Many died.

Phnom Penh – the capital city of Cambodia. In the 1970s Cambodia was ruled by a military group known as the Khymer Rouge who massacred hundreds of thousands of their fellow citizens, an act which is now recognized as genocide.

All flesh is grass – a quotation from the Bible. Isaiah, Book 40, verse 6 reads:

All flesh is grass, and all the goodliness in us the flower of the field. The grass withereth, the flower faileth, but the word of our God shall stand forever.

The First Epistle of Peter, Book 1, verse 24 uses the same phrase. Traditionally the phrase is interpreted as showing the inevitability of death and Duffy seems to be using it ironically since in the three cities she mentions many of the violent deaths are clearly avoidable.

In the first stanza the photographer is alone in his darkroom preparing to develop the "spools of suffering" that he has accumulated on his travels. The phrase "spools of suffering" is foregrounded by the alliteration and makes clear Duffy's sympathy for the suffering the photographer has captured in images. The photographer's role is given a quasi-sacred significance by the comparison with the priest "preparing to intone a mass" and the litany of place names of cities associated with violence. The photographer is performing a sacred task by going to dangerous places and making a photographic record, so that the rest of the world is informed about the awful suffering taking place in the world.

In the second stanza, the photographer gets to work – "He has a job to do". His hands did not tremble in the war zones, despite the danger he was in, but do so now – perhaps because of the delicacy of the task, perhaps because of the excitement of seeing the images emerge or perhaps because of the suffering that he remembers when he was taking the photographs. However, he is safe in "rural England" where he experiences only "ordinary pain" and where there are no land mines in the fields

…to explode beneath the feet

Of running children in a nightmare heat.

At the start of the third stanza – "Something is happening" – an image is emerging in the dark room. The photographer starts to see "a stranger's features" and this brings back memories of the real incident itself: "He remembers the cries/of this man's wife" and "how the blood stained into foreign dust". These memories and the way Duffy expresses them suggest a strong sense of compassion and empathy on the part of the photographer. The word "ghost" is important: it clearly suggests that the man is now dead, but it also describes the way the man slowly emerges as the photograph is developed.

In the fourth stanza we learn that he has developed "a hundred agonies in black and white" – with the word "agonies" encouraging sympathy and empathy on the part of the reader. But the reality of newspaper publishing brings us up sharply: we are told that from the "hundred agonies" he has photos of, the photographer's editor will "pick out five or six/for Sunday's supplements" – which completely ignores the majority of the "hundred agonies" and the tragic stories and suffering they bear witness to. The five or six photographs selected will "prick the tears" of the "reader's eyeballs", but will not disturb the comforting routine of the newspaper's readers – "the bath and pre-lunch beers".

The poem ends with the photographer on his way back to another war-zone:

From the aeroplane he stares impassively at where

He earns his living and they do not care.

Some readings of this poem are critical of the photographer: they stress that he regards his work as "a job" in the second stanza; his work is how he "earns his living"; and there is a sense, therefore, (it could be argued) that he makes his living from the suffering of others. However, this is to ignore the sacred religious imagery in the first stanza, the trembling of his hands in the second stanza and his vivid and clearly compassionate memories in stanza three. Besides, the photographer puts himself in positions of danger in order to tell the world what is going on in distant countries: he is performing a vital function in bringing to Western Europe's attention atrocities which may be occurring in other countries which are not often featured in the news.

If there is an object of criticism in Duffy's poem it is the British public who buy the newspapers that the photographs appear in. The British readership is safe in "Rural England", suffers "ordinary pain" which "simple weather can dispel". The readers' reaction to the photographs is "tears" – but they are not meaningful tears; they are part of a normal Sunday ritual squeezed in between a bath and "pre-lunch beers". The most searing indictment of the British public is in the last line where Duffy claims "they do not care" – they do not care about suffering in far-off foreign countries, despite the efforts of the war photographer to make them care.

Duffy chooses a very regular structure for this poem. There are four stanzas each of six lines with a final rhyming couplet and with lines two and three rhyming in each stanza. This structure seems to match the organized nature of the photographer's work – especially his meticulous work in the dark room, while the final rhyming couplet mirrors the certainty that the photographer and Duffy both feel that his work is worthwhile and fulfils an important function in society. It fills an important function in society because it brings public attention to conflicts and wars all over the world.

Conflict

The photographer's job takes him to areas of conflict all over the world, but he has no power to stop the conflict – but he has the power to record it and make it known to the wider world. The poem suggests that he takes photographs of the victims of conflict – which are designed to provoke sympathy in the viewer of the photograph. However, his editor has the power to reject ninety-four of the photographs and print only six – so not every story is told, not every image is seen. He is also the recorder of the misuse of power: in Cambodia and Phnom Penh where the regime was using its power to massacre hundreds of thousands of people the world did take action, but only after the efforts of journalists had brought the regime's crimes to light. Nonetheless, the poem makes clear that there is a conflict between the whole truth (as represented by the reels of photos that the photographer takes) and the tiny number that are finally seen by the public in their newspaper. There is also a conflict between the photographer's mission to bring home the truth about overseas wars and the relative indifference of the British public.

Why?

This poem:

- encourages empathy and sympathy for all those caught up in violent conflicts all over the world.

- gives the photographer an almost sacred importance because his bravery allows images of suffering humanity to reach us.

- is an indictment of the British public for whom the photographs of suffering humanity become a part of their Sunday ritual.

- demonstrates the appalling and horrific violence of war and genocide.

- shows the relative indifference of the British public to overseas conflicts.

'Belfast Confetti' – Ciaran Carson

Context

Carson was born in Belfast in 1948 and has lived there all his life. Violence and its effects are central to much of his writing – he has lived throughout the 'Troubles' - the name given to the last forty years of the history of Northern Ireland. During the Troubles terrorist groups representing both sides of the conflict attacked each other and the British Army, and planted bombs which deliberately targeted civilians too. This poem was written in 1990, but the term 'Belfast confetti' was already in use in speech and means the shrapnel (pieces of metal) placed around explosives that would fly out and injure people when the explosive was detonated or it can mean random objects made of heavy metal which rioters hurled at the soldiers or the police during riots.

There has been violence in Ireland ever since the English tried to conquer it and make it a colony in the 16th century. The most recent era of violence is known as the Troubles and flared up in the late 1960s. Tension between Catholic and Protestant communities erupted into violence and British troops were sent to Northern Ireland to keep the peace, to keep the opposing sides apart. However, because of various factors, the violence escalated and terrorist groups on both sides of the sectarian divide became involved and increasingly powerful. There were many deaths and many bombings, and the violence continued into the late 1990s. Carson was brought up in the Falls Road area – one of the most dangerous areas of Belfast.

It is dangerous to generalize about Ireland, but essentially the Catholic community favoured unification with the Republic of Ireland, while the Protestant community wanted to remain as part of the United Kingdom. More immediately, in the 1960s the Catholic community did not have equal rights because the Protestant majority dominated politics. The British government claimed the British soldiers were in Northern Ireland to keep the peace, but Irish Republicans felt they were an army of occupation

fount – this word means two things in this poem. It is a spring of water like a fountain, but it also a fount of broken type: before computers, books and newspapers were printed using metal blocks to represent each letter and piece of punctuation which were laboriously put in position by hand. These metal blocks are not unlike the pieces of metal used as shrapnel.

Balaklava, Raglan, Inkerman, Odessa, Crimea – street names in the Falls Road area which ironically recall the Crimean War – another British imperial war, you might argue. You can read more about the Crimean War in the section devoted to *The Charge of the Light Brigade* by Alfred Tennyson.

Saracen – a British army armoured personnel carrier.

Kremlin-2 mesh – a type of mesh used over the windows of Saracens and designed to protect the windows from bombs and rockets.

Makrolon face-shields – Makrolon is a tough man-made substance which protects the face but is transparent.

fusillade – a continuous discharge of guns.

Who? The poet speaks as himself.

When? During the Troubles.

Where? In the Falls Road area of Belfast.

What? The poet is caught on the streets of Belfast when a bomb is detonated. He seems to get lost in the confusion and chaos after the explosion and describes the British Army's own confused reaction to the incident.

Commentary

This is a confused and confusing poem which you may struggle to make sense of – but it is deliberately written in this way to suggest that this sort of incident is frightening and confusing and it also demonstrates the inability of language to describe adequately what is going on. The title of the poem *Belfast Confetti* is an everyday, darkly-comic term for shrapnel or for odd pieces of metal thrown at the British soldiers during riots: it is a euphemistic slang term and derives its comic edge from our usual association of confetti with weddings which are happy, joyous occasions – unlike the riot described in this poem. It becomes darkly comic because we normally associate confetti with weddings not bombings. The 'confetti' - the shrapnel - rains down on the streets of Belfast once the bomb has exploded, and continues as the rioters use odd scraps of metal to bombard the British soldiers.

In the first stanza the poet struggles to make sense of what is going on. He is caught up in a riot and then a bomb explodes, adding to the confusion. The very first word – *suddenly* – plunges us into the midst of the action. In the wake of the explosion the air is *raining exclamation marks*: this metaphor suggests the pieces of shrapnel flying through the air; the shouts and cries of people near the bomb's blast; and also the sheer sense of shock and fear that courses through the poet. Carson continues this metaphor of the shrapnel as pieces of punctuation to suggest that language and its tools – punctuation – cannot make sense of, or convey the reality of, the riot and the bomb. *This hyphenated line* becomes *a burst of rapid fire*. The poet tries to formulate a sentence in his head, but he cannot complete it – his sense of fear and panic and shock is so strong that he has lost the ability to communicate. To make matters worse, at the end of the stanza he cannot escape – everywhere is *blocked with stops and colons*.

In the second stanza the poet is lost in his home area. The tense switches to the present to give extra immediacy. He knows *this labyrinth so well*, but cannot escape. The list of street names adds to his sense of confusion. As I have already mentioned the names are highly ironic since they are named after places in the Crimea where the British Army fought; except Raglan Street which is named after Lord Raglan, the British army commander-in-chief during the Crimean War. Everywhere he finds a dead-end. The short sentences echo his confusion and also give us the sense that he is trying to move quickly in order to get off the streets to the safety of his home. Line 15 is full of references to British soldiers, but they are described in terms of their equipment – in a list like the street names – which makes them seem dehumanized and threatening. The soldiers are not presented as human and in line 16 they fire a series of questions at him – a *fusillade of question marks*. *Fusillade* is a brilliantly chosen metaphor which is appropriate since the soldiers are asking the questions, but also suggests how potentially dangerous these questions seem to the poet in his state of panic:

My name? Where am I coming from? Where am I going?

Clearly the soldiers are trying to catch the bombers and these are genuine questions which they might have asked someone running in the streets in the aftermath of a riot and a bombing, but they are more important than that. In fact, the whole poem (composed of two stanzas of equal length) is an extended metaphor which suggests that conflict destroys language and our ability to communicate normally: 'raining exclamation marks' suggests rapid shouts of fear and alarm; 'an asterisk on the map' would look like there had been an explosion on the paper; 'stuttering' obviously shows the poet cannot get his words out because of his fear, but also suggests the sound of the 'rapid burst of fire'; the alleyways are 'blocked with stops' just as full stops block the reader at the end of the sentence.; a fusillade refers to several questions being fired at the narrator but also means rapid gunfire.

Carson's sense of total disorientation, his fear and total confusion, mean that he is unsure of who he is and where he's going, so great has been his sense of shock.

Conflict

The poem enacts the conflict of the riot situation very effectively through language, the disrupted rhythm and the extended metaphor. The British soldiers are dehumanized and it is easy to see them as an army of occupation – certainly their brief interrogation of the poet causes conflict. This conflict is internalized as the poet panics and is desperate to get to the safety of his home.

Why? This poem

- uses lists, questions and short, unfinished sentences to convey an atmosphere of fear and chaos.

- shows no overt interest in the political situation, but is wholly concerned with the reactions of one frightened and confused man.

- suggests, it could be argued, through its presentation of the soldiers and the careful selection of street names which recall foreign wars, that the British Army is an army of occupation.

- uses language to suggest the inability of language to adequately convey the reality of a riot and a subsequent bomb blast.

- enacts through its language and imagery the extreme sense of shock and disorientation that the poet feels.

'The Class Game' - Mary Casey

Author and Context

Not much is known about Mary Casey, except that she was a housewife from Liverpool. Casey was a contributor to a poetry magazine called "Voices," which existed from 1972-1984. "The Class Game," published in 1979, was one of four poems of Casey's that appeared in the magazine. "Voices" published poems by working class writers. These authors were not professional poets and had no literary reputation; they were ordinary people who wrote largely about their everyday experiences. Some critics were rather snobby about "Voices," and even the academic who had started the magazine, Ben Ainsley, wrote in the introduction that "I can make no great claims for these pieces, except that they are, it seems to me, varied, interesting, freshly written, and in most cases the work of men and women taking up a pen late in life; with some qualms, though with real curiosity as to how it will turn out." This implies that he had some doubts about the 'literary value' of the work.

Ironically to call into question the value or 'literary value' of a piece of poetry is playing a different version of the class game, because it assumes that untutored, working class poets will have little of value to communicate. This commentary aims to prove otherwise.

1979 was a turning point in British politics and society. Margaret Thatcher became Prime Minister and proceeded to implement monetarist economic policies. This led to a terrible recession with very high unemployment – especially in the northern cities like Liverpool. She went on to privatise previously nationalized industries and deliberately sought industrial confrontation with the unions – firstly, the National Union of Coalminers and the teaching unions. Britain moved from a system heavily dependent on income tax (direct taxation) to a system of indirect taxation - VAT, fuel tax – taxes whish are paid by everyone no matter what their income. The rich received tax cuts, while the poor were often unemployed or saw their wages drop in real terms. From one point of view, it is not hard to see the Tory policies of the 1980s as a form of class war – aimed at the working class.

In the 21st century you often hear some people claim that we live in a classless society, but I'm not sure that is true. If anyone has ever commented on the way you speak or the words you use or where you live or the occupations your parents have or the school you go to, then they are, in effect, making a class-based comment. I am writing this in the summer of 2015 and, with another Tory government in power, the gap between the rich and the poor widening daily and food bank use continuing to rise – it is hard to see the UK as a classless society.

wince – cringe, look embarrassed

Tara to me Ma – Goodbye to my mother

corpy – a Liverpool slang term for a council house

Wirral – part of Merseyside that is regarded as posh

Toil – work

gullet – throat

docker – someone who works in the docks or in a shipyard

Who? The poem is a dramatic monologue in which the author directly addresses a member or members of the middle or upper classes.

When? 1979 – although it could be argued that the issues the poem raises are still relevant today.

Where? No specific place, but clearly centred on Liverpool.

What? Casey asks the rhetorical question "How can you tell what class I'm from?" and proceeds to answer it mainly in terms of vocabulary – the words we use – although she also defines it in terms of where people live and their occupations. At the end of the poem Casey asserts that she is proud to be working class.

Commentary

The poem opens with a confident and challenging rhetorical question; "How can you tell what class I'm from?' The narrator of the poem asserts 'I can talk posh like some' which shows that when she uses working class words she chooses to do so, though she knows how to talk 'posh'.

This is a first-person dramatic monologue reflecting on the speaker's feelings on being judged on her accent, her vocabulary, her father's job and her general social background. The speaker is clearly from the working class ('we live in a corpy') whereas she is addressing people from the middle classes who live in a 'pretty little semi' and in the Wirral, not Liverpool itself.

The poem is not divided into stanzas but it is presented as one long stanza – this suggests a sustained outpouring or outburst of anger and annoyance at being judged by her speech and her class. Separate stanzas would have impeded the flow of her emotions and thoughts as expressed in the poem. The use of the word 'game' in the title suggests very strongly that judging people on their class backgrounds is trivial and no more than as a game as far as the speaker is concerned. Alternatively it might refer to a game you play when you are people-watching – deciding what class they come from.

The poem itself might suggest the humour and fun of a game. However, the poet introduces internal rhyme – 'nose/clothes' and 'Tata/Ma' and rhyming couplets towards the end of the poem suggests that the focus of her anger and the target of her anger – the class system - is becoming more coherent and is starting to coalesce.

The short line lengths towards the end of the poem, along with the anaphora of 'and' the enjambment between the last two lines emphasize the passion and commitment the poet feels about this subject – anger, annoyance, irritation but also an exuberant pride in her background. The rhythm of the poem also contributes to the air of essential light-heartedness, but the lines get shorter towards the end of the poem which may indicate the speaker's growing anger and frustration at being judged and being labelled working class. The speaker's tone certainly becomes more confrontational as the poem progresses.

Throughout the poem Casey uses rhetorical questions to put the reader under pressure and she juxtaposes slang or colloquial words with standard English words; sometimes the slang words are used alone without their standard English equivalent; and sometimes the class differences are presented in physical form – for example, Casey asks 'did I drop my unemployment card/Sitting on your patio (we have a yard)? Or later and much more bitterly:

Or is it because my hands are stained with toil,

Instead of soft lily-white with perfume and oil?

Casey is fully aware of the adverse effect that her words will have on a certain type of middle class reader when she asks 'does it stick in your gullet like a sour plum'. Some middle class are very sensitive to class differences and would, as Casey suggests, 'wince' at the use of words like 'bog' for toilet and 'pee' for urinate.

Conflict

Conflict in this poem revolves completely around class conflict and the judgments people make based on fear of the working class or disapproval of the way they speak, or where they live or what job they do. Casey herself adds to this conflict by her accusatory tone and her proud defiance – she is proud to be working class.

In 'The Class Game' Mary Casey writes a poem which:

- sets out to confront and shock middle class readers with its use of slang and colloquial language;

- juxtaposes assumptions about working class speech with standard English;

- demonstrates and celebrates her pride in being working class;

- is essentially light-hearted in tone, but contains a bitter, accusatory edge.

- implies that class differences still exist in modern England.

'Poppies' – Jane Weir

Context

Weir grew up on the outskirts of Manchester and works as a poet, writer and textile designer. Her poetry has been highly praised. This poem was commissioned by Carol Ann Duffy along with nine other contemporary war poems in 2009, in response to the growing violence in Afghanistan and the inquiry into the invasion of Iraq. In an interview Weir commented:

I wrote this piece from a woman's perspective, which is quite rare, as most poets who write about war have been men. As the mother of two teenage boys, I tried to put across how I might feel if they were fighting in a war zone. I was subliminally thinking of Susan Owen [mother of Wilfred Owen] *and families of soldiers killed in any war when I wrote this poem.*

Armistice Sunday – the Sunday closest to November 11th, Remembrance Day, chosen because the First World War ended on November 11th, 1918.

tucks, darts, pleats – words associated with clothes and textiles.

Who? The poet speaks directly to a son who is taking leave of his mother, the narrator.

When? We are told it is three days before Armistice Sunday, but apart from that no specific time is mentioned and no specific war is mentioned which gives the poem a universal quality. It could be any war at any time and any mother bidding farewell to her son, unsure of what will happen to him. Having said that, Armistice Sunday has only been commemorated since the First World War, and the habit of wearing poppies to remember the sacrifice of dead soldiers is also a modern phenomenon, so this is a modern poem. We know it was published in 2009.

Where? The action begins at the narrator's home and ends in the local churchyard in front of the war memorial.

What? She pins a poppy on his lapel and says goodbye at the front door. Filled with memories of his childhood, she goes to her son's bedroom and then is led to the local churchyard and the poem ends with the mother gazing at the war memorial, thinking about her son.

Commentary

The opening sentence fixes the day: it is three days before Armistice Sunday. Before her son leaves the narrator pins a poppy on the lapel of the person the poem is addressed to: it is her son, but this is only confirmed by later details. Even the gender of the speaker is not made explicit, but there are strong suggestions that it is his mother – which we will explore later. Armistice Sunday commemorates all those who have died in wars, but we might note that poppies have been placed on individual war graves to remind us that every serviceman who died was an individual. The final three lines of the first stanza use language which is rich in texture and sound qualities:

I pinned one onto your lapel, crimped petals,

spasms of paper red, disrupting a blockade

of yellow bias binding around your blazer.

Alliteration on *p* gives way to alliteration on *b*, and Weir also uses assonance to give further euphony to these lines: *pinned/crimped* and *spasms/paper/blazer* and *bias/binding*. A sense of war is introduced by the word *blockade* to describe the blazer's binding.

The second stanza gives us lots of recognizable domestic details: the mother (we assume that it is the mother because traditionally it is mothers who would fuss over a son's appearance in this way) the mother uses sellotape to remove the cat's hairs from her son's clothes and smooths his collar down. The sellotape is *bandaged around* her hand – a hint perhaps that she is finding this leave-taking painful. The narrator says *I wanted* to rub noses with her son as they did when her son was younger, but she doesn't; she also had to resist the *impulse* to run her fingers through his hair. These details suggest that now her son is older she feels she cannot do these things that a parent might naturally do to their child when they are younger. So as our children grow up, it seems, we lose some of the intimacy we enjoyed when they were small children. Another detail which confirms that the son is older is probably the gelled blackthorns of his hair. He is old enough to make decisions about his appearance. The speaker clearly feels sad that her son is growing up: in lines 10 and 11 we are told she *steeled the softening of my face* and in line 18 she tells us *I was brave* – it is as if her face will soften with tears at her son's departure, but she manages to control her feelings in order not to embarrass her son – just as she has not rubbed noses with him or run her fingers through his hair.

The words she wants to say to him won't come; they are slowly *melting* in line 18. When she opens the front door the world is overflowing *like a treasure chest* and her son is *intoxicated*: leaving home may be sad for the parent but it can be a time of excitement and opportunity for the child as these words suggest.

As soon as he has gone she goes to his bedroom and releases a song bird from its cage; I don't think we are meant to see this as literal, but it probably symbolizes the speaker's son being released into the intoxicating, *treasure chest* world – a good thing despite his mother's obvious sadness at saying goodbye.

Weir then introduces a dove which leads the mother to the churchyard. The mother is still distracted: her stomach is busy and her nervousness about her son is conveyed to us in imagery drawn from textiles and the manufacture of clothes – *tucks*, *darts*, *pleats*; she is obviously distracted too because, although it is November, she has no coat and wears no gloves. Weir is a textile designer and often uses such vocabulary in her poems. However, the fact that she goes out improperly dressed is also a sign of her deep need to follow the dove and get to the war memorial.

Once in the churchyard the speaker traces the inscriptions on the war memorial while leaning against it *like a wishbone* – a simile that displays her fragility and which also raises the idea of wishes: presumably she would wish her son to be safe and happy. The dove flies above her and is described metaphorically as *an ornamental stitch*......... and then the poem ends

I listened, hoping to hear

Your playground voice catching on the wind.

And that phrase - *playground voice* – suggests the speaker's nostalgia for her son's childhood and her regret that he has to grow up. *Playground* is a word we associate with primary schools and it is clear from earlier details in the poem that he is older and has left childish things behind.

This is a beautiful and powerful poem. The very writing of the poem can be seen to be a political act, because Weir is writing about a topic (war) which is dominated by male poets, so to give a mother a voice is an important decision.

Some readers feel that the son is going off to war and that is why Weir is saying goodbye to him. I don't see the poem quite like that. Soldiers don't wear blazers; it is not a word used to describe what soldiers wear. I think Weir's son is going off to school – secondary school, perhaps even boarding school – and this poem is about a rite of passage for mother and for her son. A rite of passage is a ritual that marks a deep change in one's life: here it is all about sending your son off into the world, about not being able to rub noses with him because he is too old for that; it might contain the fear that later in the future he might join the army and his name might one day join the names on the war memorial.

And this fear of the future leads the mother to the war memorial, because on this day when she bids goodbye to her growing son, she feels real empathy for the mothers of the men listed on the war memorial. In their cases they said goodbye to their sons and never saw them again because they died in war. So the poppy on the lapel and the fact that this poem takes place three days before Armistice Sunday are crucial to the poem's impact. It is as if our commemoration of Armistice Sunday makes the speaker acutely aware of the much worse sacrifices that mothers make in times of war and this alerts her to what might happen in the future if her son ever becomes a soldier. Becoming a soldier (or whatever your child's first job might be) would also be a rite of passage and death is the ultimate rite of passage.

And what are we to make of the dove? It is a symbol of peace, but in the final stanza the metaphor used to describe it is an ornamental stitch, a stitch which is ornamental, not practical, not serving a purpose. Does this suggest that our hopes for peace will always be ornamental and never real, never realized, never practical? Does it suggest that war will always be with us, because the dove will remain ornamental? This may seem a little fanciful to you, but the First World War which led to so many monuments in British towns and churchyards was once thought of as the 'war to end all wars', but Weir is writing in 2009 when British soldiers were dying regularly in Afghanistan. War has continued to blight human history.

Conflict

In this poem the narrator has some power over her son's appearance: she pins the poppy on his blazer, but there is a conflict between her desire to keep her son safe and his possible participation in a war in the future. However, once he has left she realizes that she has no power over war – these matters are decided by governments (although the poem does not mention this). Both the poppy and the dove are powerful symbols – one of remembrance for the dead and the other for peace - and together they draw her to the local churchyard where she traces the "inscriptions on the war memorial". She leans against the memorial "like a wishbone", showing her weakness compared with the power of the memorial and the implied power of governments in the future to send young men like her son to fight in foreign countries. There is clear conflict between her maternal instinct to keep her son safe, and the danger that in the future his name might appear on a similar war memorial. In war time, the mother would lose all control over what happens to her son – and, in fact, her position in the poem is one of powerlessness.

Why?

This interesting modern poem

- allows a woman's voice to speak on the subject of war.
- uses symbols very effectively and evocatively.
- presents an inevitable rite of passage for any mother and her child.
- links this rite of passage with the commemoration of the war dead through poppies and on Armistice Day.
- uses the language of textiles to suggest the gender of the parent.
- movingly presents the way parent/child relationships change over time.
- is more powerful because the mother in the poem represses her emotions in front of her son.
- sees the growing up of children and their loss of innocence as inevitable, but sad.

'No Problem' – Benjamin Zephaniah

Author & Context

Poet, novelist and playwright Benjamin Zephaniah was born on 15 April 1958.

He grew up in Jamaica and the Handsworth district of Birmingham, England, leaving school at 14. He moved to London in 1979 and published his first poetry collection, *Pen Rhythm*, in 1980.

He was Writer in Residence at the Africa Arts Collective in Liverpool, and was a candidate for the post of Professor of Poetry at Oxford University. He holds an honorary doctorate in Arts and Humanities from the University of North London (1998), was made a Doctor of Letters by the University of Central England (1999), and a Doctor of the University by the University of Staffordshire (2002). In 1998, he was appointed to the National Advisory Committee on Creative and Cultural Education to advise on the place of music and art in the National Curriculum and in 1988 Ealing Hospital in London named a ward after him.

His second collection of poetry, *The Dread Affair: Collected Poems* (1985) contained a number of poems attacking the British legal system. *Rasta Time in Palestine* (1990), an account of a visit to the Palestinian occupied territories, contained poetry and travelogue.

His other poetry collections include two books written for children: *Talking Turkeys* (1994) and *Funky Chickens* (1996). He has also written novels for teenagers: *Face* (1999), described by the author as a story of 'facial discrimination'; *Refugee Boy* (2001), the story of a young boy, Alem, fleeing the conflict between Ethiopia and Eritrea; *Gangsta Rap* (2004); and *Teacher's Dead* (2007) .

In addition to his published writing, Benjamin Zephaniah has produced numerous music recordings, including *Us and Dem* (1990) and *Belly of de Beast* (1996), and has also appeared as an actor in several television and film productions, including appearing as Moses in the film *Farendg* (1990). His first television play, *Dread Poets Society*, was first screened by the BBC in 1991. His play *Hurricane Dub* was one of the winners of the BBC Young Playwrights Festival Award in 1998, and his stage plays have been performed at the Riverside Studios in London, at the Hay-on-Wye Literature Festival and on television. His radio play *Listen to Your Parents*, first broadcast on BBC Radio 4 in 2000, won the Commission for Racial Equality Race in the Media Radio Drama Award and has been adapted for the stage, first performed by Roundabout, Nottingham Playhouse's Theatre in Education Company, in September 2002.

Many of the poems in *Too Black, Too Strong* (2001) were inspired by his tenure as Poet in Residence at the chambers of London barrister Michael Mansfield QC and by his attendance at both the inquiry into the 'Bloody Sunday' shootings and the inquiry into the death of Ricky Reel, an Asian student found dead in the Thames. *We Are Britain!* (2002), is a collection of poems celebrating cultural diversity in Britain.

He has recently been awarded further honorary doctorates by London South Bank University, the University of Exeter and the University of Westminster. Recent books, both for children, are an autobiography: *Benjamin Zephaniah: My Story* (2011) and *When I Grow Up* (2011).

de – the

brunt - force

an – and

yu – you

dan – than

to have a chip on your shoulders – to bear a grudge about something

me – my

Mother country – Great Britain

Who? The poet speaks directly to the reader.

When? The poem has a contemporary setting.

Where? No specific location.

What? Despite having been the victim of 'playground taunts/An racist stunts', Zephaniah holds no grudges, but uses the poem to attack racism in general and racial stereotyping in particular.

'No problem' is a phrase you might hear several times in a single day; as the title of this poem it is clearly ironic, since racism and racial stereotyping clearly are social problems which have no place in civilized society. The title also shows Zephaniah's immunity to racist taunts and stunts – he is clearly proud of who and what he is and repeats 'I am not de problem' four times in the first verse paragraph, also giving it prominence as the opening line of the poem. This is repeated almost exactly in the second verse paragraph when Zephaniah writes 'Black is not the problem'. Black people in the United Kingdom are not the problem – the problem is the racist attitudes of white British people and their habit of stereotyping black people.

The first verse paragraph deals mainly with the stereotypes that white people have of black people. Zephaniah asserts 'I am branded athletic' and 'I can do more than dance – because in our stereotypical view of black people is that they are all very good at athletics and dancing, whereas it is probably the case that they have excelled at those activities because they have had opportunities to do so, while other professions remain closed to them in our society. 'Branded' is a very emotive word: in the days of slavery slaves were branded with red-hot iron with a symbol to show who they belonged to. Zephaniah seems to be suggesting that casual racial stereotyping is almost a continuation of slavery. By contrast to athletics and dancing, he asserts 'I am a born academic' and 'I a versatile', although white people insist on pigeon-holing him because of his race.

But as the title asserts – 'no problem' – he can cope with racial stereotyping although he clearly does not think it is right or fair. He is still able to 'greet yu wid a smile' and the racist taunts and stunts he has been the victim of have left him with no grudge – 'I have no chip on me shoulders'. The poem ends with a joke. It is not uncommon to hear white people speak in racist terms or say things based on racist stereotypes and finish by asserting that 'Some of my best friends are black'. Zephaniah, having asserted that he is 'versatile', cannot be pigeon-holed and that 'Black is not the problem', jokes by saying 'Sum of me best friends are white'.

This is essentially quite a light-hearted poem but with very serious issues at its core. The language Zephaniah uses is a mixture of Black British words and standard English. The Black British words assert his pride in his identity, while the standard English words show his education – he is, after all, 'versatile'. The poem uses rhyme throughout but rejects traditional punctuation, probably because it is too conventional.

Conflict

There is a clear conflict in this poem between real black people and the stereotypes we have of black people, and the poem mocks or ridicules our stereotyping of black people and argues that they cannot be pigeon-holed – they are as varied in their accomplishments as white people.

Why?

This poem by Benjamin Zephaniah:

- rejects the casual, unthinking racial stereotyping of black people by white people;

- celebrates the poet's black identity;

- is light-hearted in tone but deals with serious issues by ridiculing them.

'What Were They Like?' – Denise Levertov

Author & Context

Denise Levertov (24 October 1923 – 20 December 1997) was a British-born American poet. During the course of a prolific career, Denise Levertov created a highly-regarded body of poetry that reflects her beliefs as an artist and a humanist. Her work embraces a wide variety of genres and themes, including nature lyrics, love poems, protest poetry, and poetry inspired by her faith in God. Levertov was born and grew up in Ilford, Essex. Her mother, Beatrice Adelaide (née Spooner-Jones) Levertoff, came from a small mining village in North Wales. Her father, Paul Levertoff, had been a teacher at Leipzig University and as a Russian Hassidic Jew was held under house arrest during the First World War as an 'enemy alien' by virtue of his ethnicity. He emigrated to the UK and became an Anglican priest after converting to Christianity. In the mistaken belief that he would want to preach in a Jewish neighbourhood, he was housed in Ilford, within reach of a parish in Shoreditch, in East London. His daughter wrote, "My father's Hasidic ancestry, his being steeped in Jewish and Christian scholarship and mysticism, his fervour and eloquence as a preacher, were factors built into my cells". Levertov, who was educated at home, showed an enthusiasm for writing from an early age and studied ballet, art, piano and French as well as standard subjects. She wrote about the strangeness she felt growing up part Jewish, German, Welsh and English, but not fully belonging to any of these identities. She notes that it lent her a sense of being special rather than excluded: "[I knew] before I was ten that I was an artist-person and I had a destiny". She noted: "Humanitarian politics came early into my life: seeing my father on a soapbox protesting Mussolini's invasion of Abyssinia; my father and sister both on soap-boxes protesting Britain's lack of support for Spain; my mother canvasing long before those events for the League of Nations Union; and all three of them working on behalf of the German and Austrian refugees from 1933 onwards... I used to sell the *Daily Worker* house-to-house in the working class streets of Ilford Lane". The

Daily Worker was a Communist newspaper and in the Spanish Civil War a socialist government fought a war against fascist rebels - who won and who imposed a brutal fascist dictatorship on Spain.

When she was five years old she declared she would be a writer. At the age of 12, she sent some of her poems to T. S. Eliot, who replied with a two-page letter of encouragement. In 1940, when she was 17, Levertov published her first poem. During the Blitz, Levertov served in London as a civilian nurse. Her first book, *The Double Image*, was published six years later. In 1947, she met and married American writer Mitchell Goodman and moved with him to the United States the following year. Although Levertov and Goodman would eventually divorce in 1975, they did have one son, Nikolai, together and lived mainly in New York City, summering in Maine. In 1955, she became a naturalised American citizen and is considered an American poet. She achieved fame through a series of books which dealt with the Vietnam War.

Vietnam had been a French colony until 1954. When the French withdrew a civil war broke out between Communist North Vietnam and capitalist South Vietnam. North Vietnam's aim was to unite the country, South Vietnam's to preserve its independence. However, this took place during the Cold War and America intervened (initially with military advisers) in order to help South Vietnam and to stop the spread of Communism. However, the South Vietnamese were clearly losing the war. So in 1964 the USA began to bomb North Vietnam and in 1965 it sent 200, 000 combat troops to Vietnam. The heavy bombing of North Vietnam continued: in May 1964 the American general, Curtis Le May, said in a quotation that became notorious: "Tell the Vietnamese they've got to draw in their horns or we're going to bomb them back to the Stone Age".

As the 1960s wore on the Americans committed more and more troops to Vietnam until there were half a million there by 1968. However, although the USA was the world's military superpower and possessed military technology that was far superior to the North

Vietnamese army, it was clear that North Vietnam were winning the war by using hit-and-run guerrilla tactics and avoiding large-scale open battles with the American army.

Back home in the USA, the war became increasingly unpopular and a growing anti-war movement quickly grew and huge public protests were held. Marshall McLuhan, a cultural commentator, said in 1975:

TV brought the brutality of war into the comfort of the living room. Vietnam was lost in the living rooms of America – not on the battlefields of Vietnam.

From 1970 America began to withdraw its troops, but continued to bomb North Vietnam with its aircraft. By 1973 all American ground troops has been withdrawn, leaving only advisers. By 1975 the North Vietnamese Army seized the capital of South Vietnam, Saigon, and the war was over and the country was unified. America's military might had been humiliated.

This poem (published in 1971) is part of domestic American protest against the Vietnam War.

jade – is a semi-precious rock, usually green in colour, which is used to make ornaments and jewellery.

paddies – flooded fields in Asia used to grow rice.

epic poem – a long narrative poem which tells of brave and heroic deeds.

Who? There are two speakers: the first asks questions which form the first stanza; the second answers each question in turn and in detail. We cannot tell who the speakers are but it is clear that the first speaker holds some sort of authority or importance because the second speaker address him as 'Sir'.

When? In an imagined future in which America has won the war and completely obliterated Vietnam, its people and culture.

Where? There is no specific location.

What? The questions are asked to ascertain the truth about the Vietnamese way of life and culture.

The first question is:

Did the people of Vietnam

use lanterns of stone?

To which the answer is;

Sir, their light hearts turned to stone.

it is not remembered whether in gardens

stone gardens illumined pleasant ways.

Their light hearts turning to stone is an effect of the war. The passive voice of 'it is not remembered' is chilling here as is the implication the pleasant ways no longer exist because they have been destroyed.

The second question is:

Did they hold ceremonies

to reverence the opening of buds?

The answer is:

Perhaps they gathered once to delight in blossoms,

but after their children were killed

there were no more buds.

A response that is full of anguished empathy for the child victims of the war.

The questioner asks: 'Were they inclined to quiet laughter?' which elicits the response 'Sir, laughter is bitter to the burned mouth' – a line which manages to suggest both the physical suffering of the

Vietnamese (burned mouth) and their psychological suffering – they have forgotten how to laugh.

The next question – 'Did they use bone and ivory/jade and silver for ornament?' – elicits a longer answer:

> *Ornament is for joy.*
>
> *All the bones were charred,*
>
> *it is not remembered. Remember,*
>
> *Most were peasants; their life*
>
> *was in rice and bamboo.*
>
> *When peaceful clouds were reflected in the paddies*
>
> *and the water buffalo stepped surely along terraces,*
>
> *maybe fathers told their sons old tales.*

I have quoted this answer at length because it gives us a more complete picture of how Levertov presents the Vietnamese people in the poem: they are presented by the poet as simple, innocent, gentle people living a humble and simple existence. However close that may be to the truth is irrelevant: in the poem and in the poem's context Levertov's presentation of their way of life like this is a direct and peaceful contrast to the destructive military might of the American Army with its ability to bomb the Vietnamese into surrender. They have no epic poem, although Levertov speculates that 'fathers told their sons tales' – the past tense is significant since they no longer tell their sons tales., because they no longer exist as a people.

The final question is 'Did they distinguish between speech and singing?' The respondent says that their speech was 'like a song' and their singing 'resembled moths in moonlight' – a gentle, peaceful image. But the truth is that no one knows because 'it is silent now'. In

Levertov's imagined future, Vietnamese culture and its people have been wiped out.

The poem is written in free verse which is appropriate as the respondent struggles to give coherent answers to the questions asked.

This poem became rapidly famous when it was published in 1971. Some readers felt she was being slightly patronising to the Vietnamese – who had a fully developed cultural life and were not all simple peasants. However, that is to miss the point of the poem, I think. The poem is for an American audience and it serves as a piece of anti-war propaganda and, in contrast to the brutality of American mass bombing of North Vietnamese cities, Levertov is quite consciously trying to create sympathy and empathy for the Vietnamese.

Conflict

This poem deals with the aftermath of a conflict and, within the poem itself, there is little conflict – but it only came to be written because of the Vietnam War. We might sense a minor conflict in the poem between the dryly academic and dispassionate questions of the opening stanza, and the answering voice which is keen to provoke sympathy and empathy for the Vietnamese people. There are also oblique references to the effects of the conflict between the USA and North Vietnam: 'their children were killed'; 'the burned mouth'; 'All the bones were charred' and 'When bombs smashed those/Mirrors there was only time to scream'. And thus the second voice gives us details, designed to shock, of the conflict.

Why?

This poem by Denise Levertov:

- is set in an imaginary future (North Vietnam actually won the war and ejected the Americans);

- is a poem which protests about American tactics and involvement in Vietnam;
- arouses sympathy for the Vietnamese people;
- warns against the possible genocide of the Vietnamese people and uses chilling images to suggest that eventual fate.

Glossary

The Oxford Concise Dictionary of Literary Terms has been invaluable in writing this section of the book. I would again remind the reader that knowledge of these terms is only the start – do NOT define a word you find here in the examination. You can take it for granted that the examiner knows the term: it is up to you to try to use it confidently and with precision and to explain why the poet uses it or what effect it has on the reader.

ALLITERATION   the repetition of the same sounds – usually initial consonants or stressed syllables – in any sequence of closely adjacent words.

ALLUSION   an indirect or passing reference to some event, person, place or artistic work which is not explained by the writer, but which relies on the reader's familiarity with it.

AMBIGUITY   openness to different interpretations.

ANAPAEST   a metrical foot made up of two unstressed syllables followed by a stressed syllable.

ANAPHORA   the repetition of a word or a phrase at the start of consecutive lines of poetry, or clauses, or sentences.

ASSONANCE   the repetition of similar vowel sounds in neighbouring words.

BALLAD   a folk song or orally transmitted poem telling in a simple and direct way a story with a tragic ending. Ballads are normally composed in quatrains with the second and fourth lines rhyming. Such quatrains are known as the ballad stanza because of its frequent use in what we call ballads.

BLANK VERSE	unrhymed lines of ten syllable length. This is a widely used form by Shakespeare in his plays, by Milton and by Wordsworth.
CAESURA	any pause in a line of verse caused by punctuation. This can draw attention to what precedes or follows the caesura and also, by breaking up the rhythm of the line, can slow the poem down and make it more like ordinary speech.
CANON	a body of writings recognized by authority. The canon of a national literature is a body of writings especially approved by critics or anthologists and deemed suitable for academic study. Towards the end of the 20th century there was a general feeling that the canon of English Literature was dominated by dead white men and since then there has been a deliberate and fruitful attempt made to give more prominence to writing by women and by writers from non-white backgrounds. Even your Anthology is a contribution to the canon, because someone sat down and decided that the poems included in it were worthy of study by students taking GCSE.
CARPE DIEM	a Latin phrase from the Roman poet Horace which means 'seize the day' – 'make the best of the present moment'. It is a very common theme of European lyric poetry, in which the speaker of a poem argues that since time is short and death is inevitable, pleasure should be enjoyed while there is still time.

COLLOCATION	the act of putting two words together. What this means in practice is that certain words have very common collocations – in other words they are usually found in written or spoken English in collocation with other words. For example, the word *Christmas* is often collocated with words such as *cards, presents, carols, holidays,* but you won't often find it collocated with *sadness*. This can be an important term because poets, who are seeking to use words in original ways, will often put two words together which are not often collocated.
COLLOQUIALISM	the use of informal expressions or vocabulary appropriate to everyday speech rather than the formality of writing. When used in poetry it can make the poem seem more down-to-earth and real, more honest and intimate.
CONCEIT	an unusually far-fetched metaphor presenting a surprising and witty parallel between two apparently dissimilar things or feelings.
CONSONANCE	the repetition of identical or similar consonants in neighbouring words whose vowel sounds are different.
CONTEXT	the biographical, social, cultural and historical circumstances in which a text is produced and read and understood – you might to think of it as its background. However, it is important sometimes to consider the reader's own context – especially when we look back at poems from the Literary Heritage. To interpret a poem with full regard to its background is to contextualize it.

COUPLET	a pair of rhyming verse lines, usually of the same length.
CROSSED RHYME	the rhyming of one word in the middle of a long line of poetry with a word in a similar position in the next line.
DACTYL	a metrical foot having two unstressed syllables followed by a stressed syllable.
DIALECT	a distinctive variety of language, spoken by members of an identifiable regional group, nation or social class. Dialects differ from one another in pronunciation, vocabulary and grammar. Traditionally they have been looked down on and viewed as variations from an educated 'standard' form of the language, but linguists point out that standard forms themselves are merely dialects which have come to dominate for social and political reasons. In English this notion of dialect is especially important because English is spoken all over the world and there are variations between the English spoken in, say, Yorkshire, Delhi and Australia. Dialects now are increasingly celebrated as a distinct way of speaking and writing which are integral to our identity.
DICTION	the choice of words used in any literary work.
DISSONANCE	harshness of sound.
DRAMATIC MONOLOGUE	a kind of poem in which a single fictional or historical character (not the poet) speaks to a silent audience and unwittingly reveals

the truth about their character.

ELEGY a lyric poem lamenting the death of a friend or public figure or reflecting seriously on a serious subject. The elegiac has come to refer to the mournful mood of such poems.

ELLIPSIS the omission from a sentence of a word or words which would be required for complete clarity. It is used all the time in everyday speech, but is often used in poetry to promote compression and/or ambiguity. The adjective is elliptical.

END-RHYME rhyme occurring at the end of a line of poetry. The most common form of rhyme.

END-STOPPED a line of poetry brought to a pause by the use of punctuation. The opposite of enjambment.

ENJAMBMENT caused by the lack of punctuation at the end of a line of poetry, this causes the sense (and the voice when the poem is read aloud) to 'run over' into the next line. In general, this can impart to poems the feel of ordinary speech, but there are examples in the Anthology of more precise reasons for the poet to use enjambment.

EPIPHANY a sudden moment of insight or revelation, usually at the end of a poem.

EPIZEUXIS the technique by which a word is repeated for emphasis with no other words intervening

EUPHONY   a pleasing smoothness of sound

FALLING RHTHYM   a rhythmical effect in which the end of
the lines of a poem consist of trochees or dactyls. The effect is often of
uncertainty or poignancy, but it can also be used for comic effect.

FEMININE

ENDING   any line of poetry which ends on an unstressed
syllable and which ensures the line ends on a falling rhythm.

FIGURATIVE   Not literal. Obviously 'figurative' language
covers metaphor and simile and personification

FIGURE OF SPEECH   any expression which departs from the
ordinary literal sense or normal order of
words. Figurative language (the opposite
of literal language) includes metaphor,
simile and personification. Some figures
of speech – such as alliteration and
assonance achieve their effects through
the repetition of sounds.

FOREGROUNDING   giving unusual prominence to one part
of a text. Poetry differs from everyday
speech and prose by its use of regular
rhythm, metaphors, alliteration and
other devices by which its language
draws attention to itself.

FREE VERSE   a kind of poetry that does not conform to any
regular pattern of line length or rhyme. The
length of its lines are irregular as is its use of
rhyme – if any.

HALF-RHYME	an imperfect rhyme – also known as para-rhyme, near rhyme and slant rhyme – in which the final consonants match but the vowel sounds do not match. Pioneered in the 19th century by the Emily Dickinson and Gerard Manley Hopkins, and made even more popular by Wilfred Owen and T S Eliot in the early 20th century,
HOMONYM	a word that is identical to another word either in sound or in spelling
HOMOPHONE	a word that is pronounced in the same way as another word but which differs in meaning and/or spelling.
HYPERBOLE	exaggeration for the sake of emphasis.
IAMB	a metrical foot of verse having one stressed syllable followed by one unstressed. Lines made up predominately of iambs are referred to as iambics or iambic verse. The 10 syllable iambic pentameter (rhymed or unrhymed) is the most common line in English poetry. The 8 syllable iambic tetrameter is also very popular. The 12 syllable iambic hexameter is less common in English and is also known as the alexandrine. Even if the rhythm of a poem is predominately iambic, it does not preclude metrical variation – often with a trochaic foot at the start of a line to give maximum impact.
IDIOM	an everyday phrase that cannot be translated literally because its meaning does not correspond to the specific words in the phrase. There are thousands in English like – *you get up my nose, when pigs fly, she was all ears.*

IMAGERY a rather vague critical term covering literal and metaphorical language which evoke sense impressions with reference to concrete objects – the things the writer describes.

INTERNAL RHYME a poetic device in which two or more words in the same line rhyme.

INTERTEXTUALITY the relationship that a text may have with another preceding and usually well-known text.

INVERSION the reversal of the normally expected order or words. 'Normally expected' means how we might say the words in the order of normal speech; to invert the normal word order usually draws attention or foregrounds the words.

JUXTAPOSITION two things that are placed alongside each other.

LAMENT any poem expressing profound grief usually in the face of death.

LATINATE Latinate diction in English means the use of words derived from Latin rather than those derived from Old English.

LITOTES understatement – the opposite of hyperbole.

LYRIC any fairly short poem expressing the personal mood of the speaker.

MASCULINE ENDING Any line of poetry which ends on a stressed syllable.

METAPHOR the most important figure of speech in which in which one thing is referred to by a word normally associated with another thing, so as to suggest some common quality shared by both things. In metaphor, this similarity is directly stated, unlike in a simile where the resemblance is indirect and introduced by the words like or as. Much of our everyday language is made up of metaphor too – to say someone is as greedy as a pig is a simile; to say he is a pig is a metaphor.

MNEMONIC   a form of words or letters that helps people remember things. It is common in everyday sayings and uses some of the features of language that we associate with poetry. For example, the weather saying Red sky at night, shepherd's delight uses rhyme.

MONOLOGUE`   an extended speech uttered by one speaker.

NARRATOR   the one who tells or is assumed to be the voice of the poem.

OCTAVE or OCTET a group of eight lines forming the first part of a sonnet.

ONOMATOPOEIA the use of words that seem to imitate the sounds they refer to (*bang, whizz, crackle, fizz*) or any combination or words in which the sound echoes or seems to echo the sense. The adjective is onomatopoeic, so you can say that *blast* is an onomatopoeic word.

ORAL TRADITION the passing on from one generation to another of songs, chants, poems, proverbs by word of mouth and memory.

OXYMORON   a figure of speech that combines two seemingly contradictory terms as in the everyday terms bitter-sweet and living-death.

PARALLELISM	the arrangement of similarly constructed clause, sentences or lines of poetry.
PARADOX	a statement which is self-contradictory.
PATHETIC FALLACY	this is the convention that natural phenomena (usually the weather) are a reflection of the poet's or the narrator's mood. It may well involve the personification of things in nature, but does not have to. At its simplest, a writer might choose to associate very bad weather with a mood of depression and sadness.
PERSONA	the assumed identity or fictional narrator assumed by a writer.
PERSONIFICATION	a figure of speech in which animals, abstract ideas or lifeless things are referred to as if they were human. Sometimes known as personal metaphor.
PETRARCHAN	characteristic of the Italian poet Petrarch (1304 – 1374). Mainly applied to the Petrarchan sonnet which is different in its form from the Shakespearean sonnet.
PHONETIC SPELLING	a technique writers use which involves misspelling a word in order to imitate the accent in which the word is said.
PLOSIVE	explosive. Used to describe sounds that we form by putting our lips together such as b and p.

POSTCOLONIAL LITERATURE a term devised to describe what used to be called Commonwealth Literature (and before that Empire Writing!). The term covers a very wide range of writing from countries that were once colonies of European countries. It has come to include some writing by writers of non-white racial backgrounds whose roots or family originated in former colonies – no matter where they live now.

PUN an expression that derives humour either through using a word that has two distinct meanings or two similar sounding words (homophones).

QUATRAIN a verse stanza of four lines – usually rhymed.

REFRAIN a line, or a group of lines, repeated at intervals throughout a poem – usually at regular intervals and at the end of a stanza.

RHYME the identity of sound between syllables or paired groups of syllables usually at the end of a line of poetry.

RHYME SCHEME the pattern in which the rhymed line endings are arranged in any poem or stanza. This is normally written as a sequence of letters where each line ending in the same rhyme is given the same alphabetical letter. So a Shakespearean sonnet's rhyme scheme is ababcdcdefefgg, but the rhyme scheme of a Petrarchan sonnet is abbaabbacdecde. In other poems the rhyme scheme might be arranged to suit the poet's convenience or intentions. For example, in Blake's 'London' the first stanza rhymes abab, the second cdcd and so on.

RHYTHM	a pattern of sounds which is repeated with the stress falling on the same syllables (more or less) in each line. However, variations to the pattern, especially towards the end of the poem, often stand out and are foregrounded because they break the pattern the poet has built up through the course of the poem.
ROMANTICISM	the name given to the artistic movement that emerged in England and Germany in the 19790s and in the rest of Europe in the 1820s and beyond. It was a movement that saw great changes in literature, painting, sculpture, architecture and music and found its catalyst in the new philosophical ideas of Jean Jacques Rousseau and Thomas Paine, and in response to the French and industrial revolutions. Its chief emphasis was on freedom of individual self-expression, sincerity, spontaneity and originality, but it also looked to the distant past of the Middle Ages for some of its inspiration.
SATIRE	any type of writing which exposes and mocks the foolishness or evil of individuals, institutions or societies. A poem can be satiric (adjective) or you can say a poet satirizes something or somebody.
SESTET	a group of six lines forming the second half of a sonnet, following the octet.

SIBILANCE	the noticeable recurrence of *s* sounds.
SIMILE	an explicit comparison between two different things, actions or feelings, usually introduced by *like* or *as*.
SONNET	a lyric poem of 14 lines of equal length. The form originated in Italy and was made famous as a vehicle for love poetry by Petrarch and came to be adopted throughout Europe. The standard subject matter of early sonnets was romantic love, but in the 17th century John Donne used it to write religious poetry and John Milton wrote political sonnets, so it came to be used for any subject matter. The sonnet form enjoyed a revival in the Romantic period (Wordsworth, Keats and Shelley all wrote them) and continues to be widely used today. Some poets have written connected series of sonnets and these are known as sonnet cycles. Petrarchan sonnets differ slightly in their rhyme scheme from Shakespearean sonnets (see the entry above on rhyme scheme). A Petrarchan sonnet consists of two quatrains (the octet) followed by two tercets (the sestet). A Shakespearean sonnet consists of two quatrains (the octet) followed by another quatrain and a final couplet (the sestet).
SPONDEE	a metrical unit consisting of two stressed syllables.
STANZA	a group of verse lines forming a section of a poem and sharing the same structure in terms of the length of the lines, the rhyme scheme and the rhythm.
STYLE	any specific way of using language, which is

characteristic of an author, a period, a type of poetry or a group of writers.

SYLLOGISM   a form of logical argument that draws a conclusion from two propositions.

SYMBOL   anything that represents something else. A national flag symbolizes the country that uses it; symbols are heavily used in road signs. In poetry symbols can represent almost anything. Blake's 'The Sick Rose' is a good example of a poem which uses a symbol.

SYNECDOCHE   a figure of speech in which a thing or person is referred to indirectly, either by naming some part of it (*hands* for manual labourers) or by naming some big thing of which it is a part (the law for police officers). As you can see from these examples, it is a common practice in speech.

TONE   a critical term meaning the mood or atmosphere of a piece of writing. It may also include the sense of the writer's attitude to the reader of the subject matter.

TROCHEE   a metrical foot having a stressed syllable followed by an unstressed syllable.

TURN   the English term for a sudden change in mood or line of argument, especially in line 9 of a sonnet.

VERSE   another word for poetry as opposed to prose. The use of the word 'verse' sometimes implies writing that rhymes and has a rhythm, but perhaps lacks the merit of real poetry.

VERSE PARAGRAPH   a group of lines of poetry forming a

section of a poem, the length of the unit being determined by the sense rather than a particular stanza pattern.

VOLTA   the Italian term for the 'turn' in the argument or mood of a sonnet which normally occurs in the ninth line at the start of the sestet, but sometimes in Shakespearean sonnets is delayed until the final couplet.

WIT   a general term which covers the idea of intelligence, but refers in poetry more specifically to verbal ingenuity and cleverness.

Printed in Great Britain
by Amazon